FIFTY SHADES OF
GRACE

KAREN YVONNE DYKES, ESQ.

DEDICATION

This book is dedicated to God's Grace and its many manifestations in my life. To the love of my life, Antoine, you are the personification of grace in my life. To my parents, Bishop Richard and First Lady Adele Johnson, thank you for living a life of integrity beyond anyone else I have ever known. To my older brothers, Richard and Keith, thank you for allowing your brilliance to shine on me. To everyone who encouraged me and helped to make this book a reality, thank you. Finally, to every person that will be touched by the truth within these pages, thank you for entrusting me with your heart. I pray these revelations encourage, empower and inspire you to live abundantly.

CONTENTS

Scandal of Grace (Preface)   vi

I Am a Mess (Introduction)   1

1   The Godfather and The Gospel of Grace:
    When God makes You an Offer You Just
    Can't Refuse   5

2   Two Lines Tall   19

3   Losing My Virginity   22

4   Grace is Sufficient - Saved by Grace   28

5   Confession is Good for the Soul   36

6   The F Word   40

7   F Yourself   49

8   Perfection is an Urban Legend   54

9   His Strength is Made Perfect in My Weakness   58

10 Grace is Not a Credit Card   63

11 Falling From Grace   68

12 Grace in a Meritocracy   72

13 The Work God wants From You   78

14 Faith Cycle   83

15 First Things First   93

16 Gratified Life   101

    Conclusion   105

    God Loves You (Epilogue)   108

FOREWORD

We would like to introduce you to the author of this book. She is our youngest, third left-handed child and first and only daughter. Yes, she is the baby of our family! She was born with an unusual sensitivity and propensity to tell the truth—even knowing the consequences would be grave. Like the meaning of her name, Karen her heart is pure. Like the rest of us, she resides in a vessel of clay, but from a child she has demonstrated a sincere desire to please God. Much of her story is our story. Her journey from religious legalism to freedom in Christ has been our journey.

Fifty Shades of Grace articulately explains the powerful truth of God's extravagant love for humanity. Read this book only if you are prepared to see your chains of self-righteousness or self-loathing melted into an ocean of forgiveness and divine favor. The principles in this book operate like the law of gravity. Principles work without regard to ethnicity, education, economics, color, or creed! They work for those included and those excluded from society's honor roll. The law of the Lord is perfect, converting the soul. Let the law of grace transform you into an invincible, eternal vessel of honor! The grace of God that brings salvation will teach you.

Let the truth you learn make you free from the bondage of dutiful performance desiring to please man, to serving from a heart of delight in devotion unto God! You will no longer serve the letter of law, but serve God out of a spirit of love and reverence—worthy of the royalty ordained for each and every one of us! You are destined to reign! Jesus Christ loved us, and washed us from our sins in his own blood, and made us kings and priest unto God and His Father! Revelation 1:5-6

Bishop Richard and Lady Adele Y. Johnson, Sr. Pastors
Destiny Family Christian Center, El Paso, Texas

Scandal of Grace
(Preface)

Are you tired? Worn out? Burned out on religion? Come to me. Get away with me and you'll recover your life. I'll show you how to take a real rest. Walk with me and work with me—watch how I do it. Learn the unforced rhythms of grace. I won't lay anything heavy or ill-fitting on you. Keep company with me and you'll learn to live freely and lightly."
Matthew 11:29-30 (MSG)

Why Fifty Shades of Grace? A twist on the title of a very controversial book and movie, the title screams, "Scandal!" More than just amazing, God's grace is scandalous. His love is promiscuous. It will set you free from the bondage of perfectionism, condemnation, feelings of inadequacy and religion. God loves us indiscriminately. It does not matter what you look like or where you came from. Before you did anything good or bad, even after you did enough bad to warrant death, He loves you. I say loves instead of loved because His love is eternal. He is outside of time in eternity and can exist in our past, present and future all at once. Therefore, His love encompasses the fullness of who we are, the good, the bad and the ugly. Nothing takes Him by surprise or tempts Him to change His mind because He already knows.

God is there in the midst of our future mistakes. God is there in our past failures. God is here in this present moment in the midst of our frailty and flaws. He knows us from the inside out. He knew you before you were formed in the womb. He knows the number of hairs on your head. He knows every aspect of your being and yet He loves you! God is love. There is nothing about who you are that can change the nature of His being. There's no mistake that eclipses His love. There is not an evil intention or action that has the power to negate His informed premeditated decision to love you. That is scandalous!

What's more, God loving us in the midst of our mess challenges our notions of right and wrong, redemption and judgment. In the Old Testament, disobedience may get you stoned to death. But, when Jesus hits the scene He challenges the one who is without any sin to cast the first stone. Grace is not black and white. There is a myriad of subtleties that go beyond our human ability to discern. Grace is God's business. It is not neat and formulaic. There is no mathematical equation that can lead you to the right answer for grace every time. Grace is the gray area that exists between our guilt for breaking the law of God and God's punishment. It is the space between our unworthiness and God's determination to bless us anyway.

We do not get what we deserve in the form of punishment and separation from God because of our sin and failure. That is grace. Yet, we get what we do not deserve and cannot earn, His unmerited favor. That, too, is grace. Grace is so controversial that some may want to protest this book and burn it in a bonfire. Why? Because reading this book will set you free from the black and white idealistic rules of religion and those that would use it to control the masses, into an authentic relationship with the Creator by and through His unbounded grace. Truth will cause you to rebel from your religious conformist nature towards the true liberty and individuality that is only found in grace. However, the liberty found in grace is what gives us the power to transform into the righteousness of God in Christ Jesus.

No grace? No transformation. Sure, religion can alter our behavior. Religion calls us on the carpet and demands that we get our act together. But, only a relationship with God based on grace can transform us from the inside out. If you do not want to be set free, happy, living a rich and satisfied life through a growing relationship with Jesus Christ, then I advise you to put this book down immediately. Conversely, if you want to escape from the perfectionistic, tired, worn-out, life-sapping religion that has you frazzled, you owe it to yourself to read this in order to get a deeper understanding of the syncopated, unforced rhythm of the grace of God.

Wait, not so fast. First, let me tell you a bit about the unique layout of this book so that you know what to expect. This book is kind of an inspiration sandwich. In the center, you will find personal anecdotes from my life to help illustrate some of the principles or "shades" of grace. This section features "Grace Reflections" to help you consider your sometimes subconscious thoughts and perspectives and to apply grace principles in your life. The beginning and end of this book don't feature "Grace Reflections." Instead, they contain foundational material to help build your faith. I still want you to reflect here. But, instead of reflecting within, I hope you see the big picture of the grace of God at work in our world in the context of the Bible.

I AM A MESS
(Introduction)

I have a confession to make: I am a mess.

You may be thinking, "Yeah. And. . ." But, for me that was a devastating – DEVASTATING realization. Why? Because I am (strikethrough) *was* a consummate perfectionist, raised by two consummate perfectionists and I thought at one time that my life was going to be. . . well, PERFECT. I believed that somehow I was the exception to the rule, that I would demonstrate the type of super model existence that would stand in stark contrast to "the world" and would therefore bring God much glory and honor. I have since come to realize that nothing could be further from the truth. There is nothing innately holy about me, nothing model about the skin that I am in, nothing celestial about my flesh. Sigh. I don't think I came across as judgmental to others, but unbeknownst to me I was quite self-righteous.

Self-righteous? That couldn't be me right? I was friendly and had a warm personality. Self-righteous people were cold and snobbish. I loved to laugh and didn't think I had arrived yet. Or did I? Self-righteous people feel perfect right? Sometimes. Sometimes not. I was self-righteous in the sense that I thought my goodness was dependent on *my* goodness. In other words, I thought that it was through my own determination to do the right thing that I was right. It was essentially up to me. I am good because I do good. I am right because I do right. Therefore, if I want God to be pleased with my life, I have got to always be right. It's simple really. The only thing that I have to do to be successful, fulfill my destiny and reflect God in the way that I live my life is *be perfect*. That's it!?! Oh, I can do that. Now what should I do with my extra time? … Yeah right!

I am a mess. And, it is OK. It is better than OK. It is wonderful! I don't have to be afraid to live, to love, to make mistakes, or to (gasp) be seen as imperfect. Oh Lord! Someone call 911. Did I just say that? It is through the messy parts of life that God has shown Himself to me to be so much better than the hard core gavel-toting deity I learned about in Sunday School, the one that is ready to pass judgment and hold me in contempt. God is not like Judge Judy; He doesn't take joy in calling you an idiot and a liar, pointing out your weakness and declaring He can see right through any attempt to appear competent. No! God is not waiting for me to fall into sin so just then He can come back as a thief in the night and say, "Gotcha!" OOPS, I missed it; now I'm stuck in hell for eternity. Cue the screeching noise in *Psycho*.

That is scary. The thought of hell, no matter how abstract, is scary. Living with the haunting thought of never measuring up, never being good enough is hell in itself. But, I don't have to be afraid and neither do you. Let's let that sink in a moment. We do not have to live in fear. The perfect love of God as shown in Christ Jesus thrusts fear out like an eager little-league pitcher on the mound, only further and faster.

I have an inkling that if you're reading this, you're not perfect either. It could be that fear and anxiety has tried to strangle the enjoyment out of your life like it did mine. Just maybe, like me you are looking for a way out. I am not claiming to be a guru. But, like Harriet Tubman I have been a slave and have found a path to freedom. Having been a slave to my own expectations and the subsequent disappointments of my failure to meet them, I am on my own journey to liberty. This book is me exposing myself, at least in part, to help show you the way. In truth, we will be taking this journey together because I have not yet arrived. Everyday is both a new journey and a continuation of the path laid out for me. I am told that before the term Christian was coined, believers in Jesus were known as "followers of The Way." *The aim is not to arrive. The aim is to follow Jesus.* Claiming arrival would be akin to claiming perfection. That is not the point. That is the antithesis of the point. Living a rich and satisfying life through a genuine, intimate relationship with Jesus Christ is the point. My relationship with Jesus is growing both in spite of and because of my flaws. Through my weakness, His strength is made perfect. Through every ailment, another aspect of His healing power is revealed. What you are about to read has helped me. I wrote it because I believe it can help you too!

If you're ready to be free, read on! However, I must warn you: It is hard to break free of old habits and ways of thinking, especially when there are forces both natural and spiritual that have conspired together to keep you bound. There are entire multi-billion dollar industries that are dependent on you feeling like you're not quite good enough "as is." In some ways, the entire consumerist western economy is dependent on you establishing your worth in your effort and the things you amass. This idea of a meritocracy is built into the core of American culture and feeds our tendency to feel like we must use every bit of our energy in order to justify our existence and earn our worth. The meritocracy math goes something like this:

Less Effort = Less Worth = Worthless.

So we strive our entire lives to prove that we are not worthless. Like a hamster on a wheel, we just keep running hoping to catch up to the standard set by the real housewives of fill in the blank. Let me ask you a question. How much does it take to be worthy? How much effort does it take to be established as a valuable, deserving human being? Can you ever reach a worthiness threshold or is it constantly before you like the pot of gold at the end of the rainbow? What are you working for? Really contemplate those questions. Maybe you don't consider yourself a perfectionist. You are not a Type A personality. However, you may find that contemplating these questions reveals a subconscious struggle that has been impeding your enjoyment of life. This is less about personality and more about the driving force of your life, the thing at your back that is pushing you to make the choices that you do.

This book is not an invitation to become a hippie and abandon the long-standing values of hard work and achievement. It is an effort to make you cognizant of what it is you're working for and distinguish it from where it is you are working from. This book is an invitation to take up arms and wage war against the forces that would collude together to keep us from experiencing God's present best for our lives: freedom, peace, joy, love, success, happiness, contentment, healing, authentic relationships, etc. I say present best because we often lie to ourselves, telling ourselves that it will be better when... (Fill in the blank happens.) It will be better when I finally get it right; when I get married; when I get divorced; when I have children; when my kids move out; when I get the degree; when I get the job; When I've proven myself at work; when I get another job I like better... Unless we have a Delorean equipped with the ability to take us back to the future and our past, we must declare our independence, stop walking in one-day-when and start walking in now!

All you have is now. Period. Your life is not around the corner it is right here, right now. However, you are presently living, is your life. I know you have goals, dreams, aspirations or at least you want to and you see something better for yourself upon the manifestation of those things into reality. That's awesome. *But, if you die today, you will not be held accountable for your tomorrow, you will be held accountable for your now.*

"Now faith is the substance of things hoped for, the evidence of things not seen." Hebrews 11:1 (NKJV). **You can live in the substance of your hopes and dreams before they manifest.** That joy and sense of fulfillment that you are putting off until you arrive is something you can have in the present. That sense of self-worth that you expect to feel upon your achievement does not have to wait. You can walk worthy right now. The life that you live in the present, the now life, can be evidence of what is to come.

I don't know about you, but that's what I want. Joy now on the way to more joy. Peace now on the way to more peace. Love now on the way to more love. Happiness now on the way to a greater manifestation of happiness! I believe that the only way to legitimately have that kind of life is by embracing the magnificent, magnanimous grace of God. To be clear, this book is not about me. This book is about Jesus, grace personified. It is my highest aim to help you see Jesus more clearly by painting a picture of grace that you probably have never seen before. Getting this understanding of grace and actually applying it to your everyday life is a sure-fire way to make every day better, every single day. But, it is easier said than done. Moment-by-moment we must bring our internal thoughts into alignment with the truth of His grace. As we do, those moments get better; then those days get better; then our life gets better! I want to live my best life and I am convinced the way to do it is through grace. If you are with me, let's go!

CHAPTER ONE:

THE GODFATHER &
THE GOSPEL OF GRACE:
WHEN GOD MAKES YOU AN OFFER
THAT YOU JUST CAN'T REFUSE

Did you know that the words grace and faith were used in everyday language before Christianity even became a thing? Did you know the practices that those words spoke to at one time pervaded the so-called secular life of those living in the Roman empire and surrounding lands in antiquity? I bet you did not realize that you can learn more about Jesus watching the classic American film, The Godfather, than you probably could in a month of Sundays? Maybe that's an exaggeration. Then again, depending on where you attend church, maybe it's not.

It was the discovery of this truth that made me start writing this book. At the urging of an acquaintance, I put myself in it and exercised vulnerability so that folks would not be bored by raw information. It may be a little heady. But, trust me; it is worth the investment of your intellectual capital to get the guaranteed dividends of understanding. This is going to take your understanding of grace to a whole new level. I pray that in turn, your faith in Jesus and determination to walk in the truth of His grace is multiplied many times over.

I am a lawyer. Not to say that is the thing in which I base my identity. I mean as opposed to being a theologian. I just had to look up how to spell theologian. I am neither an anthropologist nor a sociologist whose expertise is ancient culture.

I'm just a lawyer who despite being licensed in Texas and California is working full-time as a youth pastor / media director / worship leader in a church founded by my parents when I was eight years old.

I have spent my entire life in church, and yet I still come across revelatory truth that changes my whole perspective on what the Gospel of Jesus Christ really is all about. I cherish these moments when listening to a book or sermon and discovering something that shines the light of truth on who this man Jesus really is. My pulse gets faster. My mind races. My soul is set ablaze. My eyes get a bit watery and my heart fills with gratitude as I come to know that He is so much better than I ever realized! What had I been thinking all this time? I really didn't get it until right this moment and I want so much more!

This writing was birthed out of such an aha! moment. (I'm an Oprah fan and I couldn't resist.) Grace is the foundation of what we believe as Christians. It is an easy concept to understand, but tough to truly grasp. Unmerited favor. What's that? Oh, so Jesus provided something for me that money cannot buy and no amount of good deeds could earn. All I have to do is put my faith in Him and I have no worries because my after-life insurance policy is in place at Heaven & Co. More than insurance, I have blessed assurance. Sweet!

But, is faith just a head nod to the concept of Jesus dying for our sins akin to liking a picture on your Instagram feed? That's a good look; it meets my approval . . . double tap for you! Is it like accepting a gift from a guy you don't even like? Thanks for the roses Julian, but I am washing my hair Saturday night. If you are really honest (and if you have ever really let yourself think about it) it seems that there must be something more to the story. Grace sounds awesome, too good to be true even, but is that the whole story? I contend that there is indeed more imbedded in the concept of grace than what my thirty (mumbling) years in church have ever revealed until a couple years ago when I had a moment of revelation, more than what my American mind would ever imagine, more than what I have heard any of my favorite preachers say.

Don't get me wrong. This is nothing new in the grand scheme of things. In secret academic theologian chambers, it is probably discussed with regularity. I wouldn't know because I've never been in a secret academic theologian chamber. But, I did listen to a book that mentioned the concept by E. Randolph Richards and

Brandon J. O'Brien called, *Misreading Scripture Through Western Eyes*. Hmm, that is interesting, I thought. I have got to look into that. Then, when I was considering what to preach to the youth as a part of our Jesus Is _____ series (shout out to Judah Smith) it hit me. GRACE. I need to go back and research that thing I heard. It changes everything. So I did. And, WOW!

I ran across a blog that lead me to an eye opening article originally published in the Ashland Theological Journal in 1999. Patronage and Reciprocity: The Context of Grace in the New Testament written by David A. deSilva. Unlike me, deSilva has a Ph.D. from Emory University and at the time of the writing was an Associate Professor of New Testament and Greek at Ashland Theological Seminary. The Article is filled with academic references to Roman historians, Jewish sages, and the like. If you are a geek like that and want to follow the reference rabbit trail, please access the article and do just that. I do not intend to re-prove the cultural premise that he masterfully articulated there. What I am attempting to do here is to simply take the concepts synthesized by deSilva and speak them in a down-to-earth way that will hopefully set your soul on fire like it did mine. If you are already a Christian, get ready to love Jesus more, to receive His love in a greater way, to double down on your commitment to following him. If you are a skeptic, I hope this opens up your eyes to see the truth within the Gospel of Grace and causes you to begin your own journey of faith.

No one has time to waste so I will hit you with a quick one-two punch and you will be done with this book before you know it. Are you ready to read the Bible in a radically enlightened way? Are you prepared to live a life of purpose, inspired by grace? Are you in good enough health for it to be safe when your heart begins to race while discovering the hidden truth in the pages to come? If so, I invite you to read on. If not, you can still keep reading if you want to. Let us begin with a few key words that are pivotal to your expanded understanding the grace concept.

The Godfather

You may or may not have seen this classic piece of American cinema about an Italian dynasty led by their iconic patriarch, Don Corleone, respectfully referred to as, "Godfather." There is a scene in the film that really encapsulates the essence of who Don Corleone is and how he relates to the world around him. I painstakingly watched the scene and transcribed it because I want you to get what I'm talking about. Set on the backdrop of a huge wedding celebration, a groveling man comes to Don Corleone for help in obtaining justice after the court-system left him disappointed. It goes like this:

Bonasera: I, I went to the police like a good American. These two boys

were brought to trial. The judge sentenced them to three years in prison and suspends the sentence. Suspend the sentence!? They went free that very day! I stood in the courtroom like a fool. And those two bastards, they smiled at me. Then I said to my wife, "For justice, we must go to Don Corleone."

Don Corleone: Why did you go to the police? Why didn't you come to me first?

Bonasera: What do you want of me? I'll do anything. But, do what I beg you to do.

Don Corleone: What is that?

Bonasera rises from his chair and whispers in Don Corleone's ear.

Don Corleone: That I cannot do.

Bonasera: I'll give you anything you ask.

Don Corleone: We've known each other many years, but this is the first time you came to me for counsel or for help. I can't remember the last time you invited me over your house for a cup of coffee even though my wife is godmother to your only child. But, let's be frank you never wanted my friendship and uh you were afraid to be in my debt.

Bonasera: I didn't want to get into trouble.

Don Corleone: I understand. You found paradise in America, had a good trade, made a good living, police would protect you and there were courts of law. And you didn't need a friend like me. But, eh now you come to me and you say, "Don Corleone give me justice." But, you don't ask with respect. You don't offer friendship. You don't even think to call me Godfather. Instead, you come into my house on the day my daughter is to be married and you ask me to do murder for money.

Bonasera: I ask you for justice.

Don Corleone: That is not justice. Your daughter is still alive.

Bonasera: Then they will suffer then as she suffers. How much shall I pay you?

Don Corleone: Bonasera. Bonasera. What have I done to make you treat me so disrespectfully? If you had come to me with friendship, then the scum that ruined your daughter would be suffering this very day. And if an honest man such as yourself should make enemies, then they become my enemies. And then they would fear you.

Bonasera: Be my friend. (Bowing down.) Godfather.

Godfather: Good. Someday and that day may never come I'll call upon you to do a service for me. But, until that day, accept this justice as a gift on my daughters wedding day.

And scene.

That's good right!? Maybe you should google it so you can watch it for yourself. What we see in this scene is a more contemporary example of the social structure that existed during the time that the New Testament was being written. The social system of that day was known as patronage.

Patronage

This is where it really gets good. What we just saw in the scene from The Godfather is a somewhat warped derivative of an ancient socioeconomic culture that was pervasive throughout the Roman empire. In ancient Rome, an elite few controlled most of the property, wealth and power. Hmm, that sounds strangely familiar. Anyway, you could get the basics at the market. But, there were no credit cards, no farm subsidies, no student loans. Your average Josephus on the street could not just write a letter to his senator to see reforms made in the neighborhood. They couldn't Wikipedia their problem to research a solution. No. No. No. They did not have access. They were locked out. You could not fill out an application and be impartially chosen for a position based on your resume and educational background. Who says you can even get an educational background? You needed a relationship with someone who could make those things happen for you, someone who could grant you favor. That someone was a patron. In The Godfather, the patron would be... You guessed it! Don Corleone. What a powerful figure! Just about anything could be accomplished through his authority and influence.

Favor
The requested favor was something that money could not buy, services could not earn and no patron was obligated to provide. It was only given out of the good will of the patron, out of his or her willingness to show favor to the petitioner for the petitioner's benefit alone with no expectation of personal advantage for themselves. The idea is that this gift is an altruistic expression of the loving kindness of the patron, akin to the gods. It is a free gift. No strings attached. If a patron granted a petition, the petitioner became a client, graciously referred to by the patron as friend. This would be the beginning of a long mutually beneficial relationship where goods and services were exchanged.

In the scene from The Godfather, the favor requested could not be bought with money. No service would have earned Bonasera the right to his request. He wanted something above and beyond what he could acquire on his own, no matter how many hoops he jumped through or how much success he achieved. The only way he could get "justice" was by endearing himself to someone who could carry it out on his behalf. We see the indignant response of Don Corleone when Bonasera tries to treat the request as though it was on the open market. "How much will it take? I'll do whatever you ask." No sir! Your money and anything you could offer are wholly inadequate to get you what you're asking for. The only way to get it is to obtain the good-will of the Godfather.

But, like me and many of us reading this, Bonasera is an American and proud of it. He has fully bought in to the American dream and is used to operating in a seemingly impartial system where he can earn or has a right to what he wants. Bonasera had established a business, raised a family, made a name for himself.

10

He did not want the perceived hassle of being in relationship with the Godfather. He didn't need the Godfather because he could do it all on his own: File a police report. Prosecute the case. Trust the process. After all, it is based on objective principles right?

But what happens when those objective principles lock you out of possessing what you hope for? There is no objectively evaluated application to fill out to get favor. It s just given. And the favor is not a reflection of the petitioner and what he may or may not deserve; it is a reflection of the one granting it. Don't get it twisted. This is not a meritocracy. This is not a one-off, hit it and quit it kind of transaction. This is a relationship. It begins with acknowledging the Godfather as such, understanding that he has power that you do not possess, you cannot by any means force his hand. The favor is not for sale; it is a free gift. Period. But, even while the gift is free and freely given of the patron's own volition, the only way to receive it is by being willing to offer your friendship in exchange.

Gratitude

Wait a minute. I said it was a free gift and then I said there was an exchange. What's up with that? It is simple really, but worlds apart from the way the average westerner thinks today. While the patron idealistically gives the gift as an expression of his own good will without any expectation of a personal benefit, the social order required that the recipient have an entirely different mindset. Think about it. You just received a gift that money can't buy, you can't earn and the giver had no obligation to provide. How do you respond? According to societal norms, you should respond with gratitude. Gratitude in this context is a STRONG word. It's far more than just a thankful feeling, more than a head-nod to the hand up. It is a deeply embedded cultural duty that had at least three definitive components.

First, in order to demonstrate their gratitude to the patron, a client was expected to use whatever means they had to make the patron famous (or more famous) by publicly conferring honor to the patron, testifying to the gift and the benevolent character of the giver. Second, the client was to be loyal in their support of and affiliation with the patron, even when said affiliation was inconvenient. Third, a client was to look for any opportunity to give back to the patron by performing a service or giving a gift. All of this, while formalized in the culture, was unforced and unspoken. The last thing a client wanted was to be perceived as is ungrateful.

After all, what is going to happen the next time they need a favor if they have a reputation as an ingrate? Still, all these facets of the clients' response were not to be born out of a dreaded sense of obligation, but rather to flow freely and naturally from a true heart of gratitude. As the gift is being given, the recipient should simultaneously be so grateful that he is considering ways give back, not because he has to, but because he wants to.

This romantic notion of a gift given without expectation had been lost by the time we get to the Godfather. He makes it known, "Someday, and that day may never come, I'll call upon you to do a service for me. But, until that day, accept this justice as a gift on my daughters wedding day." Nonetheless, Bonasera is so grateful at that moment that in his mind being at the Godfather's service is the least he could do in exchange for this gift.

Entourage

One thing I have yet to expound upon is the overall benefit of being associated with a patron. The spoils in this long term relationship went far beyond the initial favor asked. The entire community would know that a client and his family were affiliated with a given patron. As such, many of the perks enjoyed by the patron because of his status would trickle down to his client friends. Perhaps a workplace bully would think twice before pushing the client friend around because the bully would know that an enemy of his becomes an enemy of his patron. Maybe the merchant in the market place who once treated the client as though he wasn't worth the time of day would suddenly perk up and stand at attention to provide him with the type of service and special prices reserved for his VIPs. It's even feasible that some of the client's peers would come to them asking for advice or help because their relationship with the patron gave them access to things beyond that of most folks in the neighborhood.

Thus the reputation of the patron increased the reputation of his client friends. Some of the favor and honor in the community held by the patron would rub off on the client like glitter, causing the client's face to sparkle a little. These were the perks of being a part of the patron's entourage. Thus, loyalty was everything. If your relationship with the patron was broken, so ended your unending gift-bag of goodies that came with being a friend. However, just as the client's enemies would become the patron's, the opposite would also be true.

Enemies of the patron would transfer their hate towards the client. And what happens when a patron goes from being hailed to nailed? Likewise, public opinion of the client would wane. Affiliation was not all sweet tarts and cotton candy. Nonetheless, the common notions of decency made it imperative that the client remain loyal even in the bad times. What wise patron would pour out his loving kindness, sacrificing time and money, freely investing in a client that was here today, gone tomorrow? For the benefits to hold firm, the relationship must hold firm. For the relationship to be solid, the commitment must be solid.

We got a glimpse of this principle when Don Corleone said, "If you had come to me with friendship, then the scum that ruined your daughter would be suffering this very day. And if an honest man such as yourself should make enemies, then they become my enemies. And then they would fear you." On the other hand, Bonasera recognized that being a friend has weight. If the Godfather is in trouble, then potentially so is the client. So Bonasera tried to avoid being in need of the Godfather's favor, lest he inconvenience his modern American life. But, sooner or later we all need a little help from someone who is stronger and more powerful than ourselves.

Grace for Grace

John bore witness of Him and cried out, saying, "This was He of whom I said, 'He who comes after me is preferred before me, for He was before me.'" And of His fullness we have all received, and grace for grace. John 1:15-16 NKJV

It is within the framework of this somewhat complex social structure that we see terminology such as grace and faith used without any religious connotation. In fact, this system that was a part of his readers' everyday lives is exactly what Paul was referencing when writing to various churches during the New Testament era. When they heard these terms, it related to their common place customs and daily reality. There were things that Paul could leave unsaid with the understanding that the common cultural practices would fill in the blanks. Lacking this background heretofore meant that I lacked an important nuance of the gospel of grace. Understanding this shines light on the the relationship between God and man that was forged through Jesus in a way that excites me. It reignited my passion for the good news about Jesus. I believe it will do the same for you!

Hear this and understand it with your entire being: **There is no grace without relationship.** The amazing thing about the word grace is that it describes the patron - client relationship and all of the associated social mores in a single word. Grace is the big picture of this mutual exchange. Moreover, (I'm talking like a lawyer now) grace describes more than the sum of these parts, the term is also used to indicate the individual parts as well. The Greek word used in the New Testament for grace is charis and connotes a grace/gift. Some versions of the Bible translate it as loving kindness. There are three facets of grace within the context of patronage culture.

First, grace refers to the willingness of the patron to provide an unmerited gift to the client. It is the pleasant disposition of the patron towards the future recipient that opens up the channel through which any specific benevolent act or gift will flow. It is the showing of favor. It is the precursor to granting any request. It is an attribute of the patron's character, his very nature. It stands alone without any compulsion or obligation. It is loving kindness. **Grace is love.**

More than just the good will of the patron, grace is the corresponding action. Grace is the benevolent act or altruistic gift that is conferred solely for the benefit of the recipient with no thought of advantage to the giver. The patron's loving kindness is demonstrated by his giving, whether it be in the form of service or material goods. **Grace is giving.**

Finally, the term grace was used to refer to the response of the client to receiving grace. That over-the-top exuberant public gratitude to the patron for his gift is grace. This response, like the nature and giving of the patron, is not coerced and is unforced. It is the natural result of a heart overflowing with thankfulness, guided in its expression by the social mores of the day. The heart of the client is so filled with gratitude that he must find a way to communicate that gratitude to the patron and the world. **Grace is gratitude.**

So in this system of grace, a patron has grace towards a client, gives grace to the client; and in turn, the client responds with grace. What!?! This was brand new to me. It's as though grace has an echo. The patron stands on the precipice of a canyon and shouts, "GRACE!" and without delay reflections of his voice return to his ear, "Grace! Grace! Grace!" Every time grace is called out, grace responds.

What this means is that grace is more than just the unmerited favor performed by the patron. One sided grace is incomplete. The concept of grace includes receiving grace and responding to grace with grace. If the grace response is left out, grace is disgraced. Did your spirit just leap? Mine did.

The Ultimate Patron

I can still feel the rush of shame and embarrassment, the sick feeling in my stomach that came over me, the blood draining from my face. I felt absolutely helpless. I was wronged, a child victim of the insecure heart of an educator. It happened during my seventh grade Spanish class at Desert View Middle School. My teacher, was Mrs. _____ (I totally feel like calling her out; but, I know that is not the wise

thing to do.) Her classroom was in a portable and the walls were covered in Joe Montana posters. One day, a student randomly proposed this hypothetical scenario, "What if Joe Montana and your husband got in a fight over you?" The class erupted with energy, giggles, side comments here and there.

I proclaimed with a smile, "You'd probably be saying, 'Go Joe! Go Joe!'" The comment was completely innocent. I was not trying to insult her or insinuate there were problems in her marriage. I just thought, being the super fan that she was, she would love to be with Joe Montana. To this day, I am not sure how or why her mood changed so sharply in that instant. She looked at me with what we used to call the "evil eye" growing up. She squinted her eyes, giving me a cold stare and declared in front of the whole class, "No boy would ever fight over you Karen." The class grew quiet. I was instantly humiliated. Why would she say something like that?

For whatever reason, she was uncouth enough to say it out loud. But, doesn't that sound like the voice of the enemy in your mind? "No boy would ever fight over you" equals "You are unworthy of love." "You are inadequate." "You've made too many mistakes." "You're too messed up." "You're just not good enough." "You don't deserve the promotion." "You deserve for her to treat you that way." However, none of those things are true. How do I know this? Because God loved you enough to send Jesus. Not only did Jesus fight for you, He died for you. You are more than worth it. You are to die for!

15

When we were utterly helpless, Christ came at just the right time and died for us sinners. Now, most people would not be willing to die for an upright person, though someone might perhaps be willing to die for a person who is especially good. But God showed his great love for us by sending Christ to die for us while we were still sinners. Romans 5:7-8(NLT)

God showed how much he loved us by sending his one and only Son into the world so that we might have eternal life through him. This is real love—not that we loved God, but that he loved us and sent his Son as a sacrifice to take away our sins. 1 John 4:9-10(NLT)

For this is how God loved the world: He gave his one and only Son, so that everyone who believes in him will not perish but have eternal life. John 3:16(NLT)

God the Father is the greatest patron of all time! Everything that He gives is a reflection of His own magnanimous character. Do not get it twisted; we do not deserve His loving-kindness. We could never earn it. It cannot be bought, no matter the price. God the Father is gracious to us simply because He desires to be. As the creator of the universe, the only reason why grace even exists is because He set it into motion. Let's trace some of the key elements of a patron and compare them to our Heavenly Father.

I first pointed out that grace refers to loving kindness, the willingness of the patron to provide an unmerited, unearned, undeserved gift to the client. Love is grace. The next facet of grace is the gift itself. Giving is grace. Those scriptures show how God the Father fulfilled these key indicators of grace to the extreme.

Hallelujah! God the Father loves us without our deserving it. That is grace! God demonstrated His love by giving His only Son in the midst of the height of our undeserving state. We could not do anything for God. So the gift of His Son was freely given without any misgivings of our worthiness or expectation of return. The King James Version says it this way, "For God so loved the world that he gave his only begotten son…" Hear this and hear it well. God does not just love you. He so loves you.

Let's be honest. Love, at least in our human experience, can sometimes get stale. Maybe you started out "in love." In love is that red hot fire, I can't stop thinking

16

about you, you are flawless to me kind of love. Then, overtime in a best-case scenario that in love feeling usually turns to just good old love. Maybe as a survival mechanism we cannot maintain that high state of alert that exists in the "in love" phase. How are you supposed work and live long term with your mind constantly distracted? So "in love" turns to "just love" for us.

However, God has an immeasurable capacity. It goes on and on; it is even more vast than the expansion of the universe He spoke into existence. Therefore, God's love has no cooling off period. He so loves you. That means He is so in love with you and it is never going to change. He will never love you less than He does right now. Conversely, He can never love you more than He does at this very moment. How can I say that? Because His love is so full and complete, so perfect that it cannot be increased. He so loved you in your worst state. He is in eternity and already knows the worst mistake you will ever make in time, even if you have not

made it yet. And yet, He declared throughout the ages that He so loves you. Words weren't enough to communicate His so love so He wrapped the Word in flesh and He moved right into our neighborhood. The most precious Word lived and ate among us, turned water into wine, made blind men see, raised the dead and was rewarded with the humiliation of the cross. God did all of this just to prove His extraordinary unfailing love, to show that our mistakes and failures are wholly inadequate to in any way interrupt His magnificent love. 1 Peter 1:2 and Revelation 13:8 tell us that this plan to sacrifice Jesus was already in place before the world even began! So before God spoke, "Let there be light," He already was fully aware of how we would need to be rescued from ourselves. Before the first sunrise, God the Father had already generously given his only son as ransom for our souls. He provided the solution before we ever sinned because He knew we would sin and He was determined to love us through it all!

There is no grace without relationship.

That means He so loves you at your best and He so loves you at your worst. But, even at our best we do not deserve this perfect love. We could never earn it. Neither Oprah nor Bill Gates could buy it. God the Father so loves us simply because He chooses to in His sovereignty. It is that kind of love that paved the way to the ultimate expression of grace, Jesus Christ. Grace is the gift. Jesus is the highest expression of grace. Jesus is grace personified. God the Father gave Jesus. Jesus gave His life. God gives eternal life to everyone that believes in Jesus. Jesus is the grace-gift that keeps on giving! Yet, in the height, depth, width and length of His love that passes knowledge, even in light of the greatest expression of love in the history of man, there is something missing in the call of grace without the response of our heart. Through His unfailing love and most precious gift, God wrote the melody and gave us the lyric. Our hearts must do the singing. But, how can we join in the chorus of His children in a gratitude song if we don't first receive His love and grace? How can we accept the gift when our minds are clouded with misbelief and shame? That is what we must deal with, the misperception of grace that causes us to miss the life-altering benefits that come with it.

In college, a young suitor showered me with gifts that included a beautiful diamond and sapphire tennis bracelet. I did not really want to be in a relationship with him so the gifts made me feel guilty. I tried to deny them. I tried not to accept them. But, he wouldn't take them back. Next, I had to choose what I would do with the gifts. Would I put them away and live as though I never received them? Or, would

I just be grateful and incorporate them into my life? After all, it was a beautiful bracelet. Likewise, we must decide what to do with our Heavenly Father's love and the gift of Jesus Christ.

Unlike a bracelet or a purse, you cannot accept Jesus without entering into a relationship with the creator. That is what it means to accept Him, to enter into a relationship with the divine lover of your soul. Fortunately, unlike that dude from college, there is no reason not to want that relationship. His love is perfect. Unfortunately, our imperfection, fear and misgivings cause us to reject this perfect love at least in part, if not in its entirety. It is time to get over ourselves, receive His loving-kindness, and allow Him to give us life! He wants to give you abundant life, a rich and satisfying life, a happy life! But, you have to receive it. You have to live and move and breath in that life. That is how you show your gratitude. By walking in the perfect liberty wherein Christ has set you free. That requires trust. We must trust Him, His love for us, the power of His gift, more than we trust ourselves and our propensity to fail.

CHAPTER TWO

TWO-LINES TALL

It was only second grade and I already hated school. I blame perfectionism, which lead to performance anxiety. After all, I needed to make all A's and that is a lot of pressure. It's not that my parents told me I had to make all A's. It's something I told myself. More on that later. I hated school; but, I loved my teacher. Mrs. Gardener was a tall, older white lady with short salt and pepper hair. She was kind and came across as polished and sophisticated to my seven-year-old self. I was smart, one of the smartest in the class, at least that was my self-concept at the time. And, I took pride in being one of the teacher's pets.

Spelling test time! Yes!!! I was one of those kids who was excited to take tests so I could show how much I knew. Please don't hate me. My mom helped me study the night before and I was good to go. Oblivious to the potential offensive stereotype gracing the cover, I grabbed my deep red, Big Chief Writing Tablet with the perforated tan paper that had both blue and red lines, extra wide so our manual dexterity had a chance to develop.

You are more than worth it. You are to die for!

"Number your paper two-lines high, skipping a space in between," Mrs. Gardner announced. 1. 2. 3. 4. 5. . . 20. I have my fat, heavy #2 pencil in hand and I'm ready. "Dream." D-R-E-A-M. That was easy. "Clean." C-L-E-A-N. Oh no. We have a problem Houston. The bottom of my letters in dream were touching the top of my letters in clean. This does not look right. OH NO! I had labeled two-lines high, but I forgot to skip an extra line between the two. This is a disaster! There is no

19

way this can go well. I am only on the second word and my chances at perfection are ruined!!! This test is a mess.

With each word slightly touching the word above it, I became more and more broken as the test progressed. By the end, I was in tears. It was time to turn it in and I began sobbing, "I want to do it over! I want to do it over! I messed up! I didn't skip a line. I want to do it over!" "It's OK Karen," Mrs. Gardener tried to reassure me. "I can still read it. It's OK." "Look. You only misspelled one." I eventually dried my tears. But, it wasn't OK. I messed up. It was messy. I wanted to do better. I had let myself down. And on top of all that, I misspelled a word!

That experience was painful enough to still be etched in my 37-year-old brain. Can you believe the way I put all of that pressure on myself at such a young age? I can. That is pretty much what I have been doing to myself my entire life! Maybe you do it too, hold yourself to standards that are unrealistic. Then, when those standards are not reached you beat yourself up for having failed, each experience robbing you of self confidence along the way until the pockets of your esteem are filled with nothing but lint and sand from the desert of your emotions.

Maybe, like my second-grade-self, those disappointments lead to tears. But, more likely they lead to your being defined and confined by fear. Think about it. If you have to be perfect, and stretching beyond your comfort zone threatens your perfection, why would you ever try that new thing? No way! Better to be safe than sorry and stay right here in my fish bowl where I know I can do it. Your world continuously shrinks according to your "Perfection Zone." Cue the Twilight Zone music in your head and read it again. Perfection Zone… Zone…. Zone...

What's more, maybe you miscalculated a life decision or two and things did not line up as you expected. Are you discounting your entire life, all of your effort and the beauty God placed inside you just because life got a little messy? Our God has enough grace to read between the lines of our mistakes and see the intention of our heart. Jesus has the power to renumber the pages of our life and turn the messes that we made into unexpected blessings. However, we have to receive Him and the grace to be human and make mistakes. Without it, all of your messes and failed tests will cripple you and leave you incapable of enjoying your life.

God does not just love you. He *so loves* you.

1) Are you internally grieving from some past or ongoing disappointment?

2) Has that hidden pain caused you to shy away from further attempts at success or forming new relationships?

3) Have you allowed some past experience to define or confine you in your own mind?

CHAPTER THREE:

LOSING MY VIRGINITY

I am a "PK." That's short for pastor's (or sometime preacher's) kid. Fortunately, my parents are the real deal. They have such integrity and commitment to their convictions that I have never seen them really blow it. Sure I have seen them get angry or argue. But, none of the big sins. No lying, cheating, sexual sin, etc. In fact, my mom married my father right out of her parents' house when she was just 18 years old. It's like she didn't even have time to sin! Growing up, one of my core desires was to see the will of God manifest in my life. Unfortunately for me, somehow that translated into a need to be perfect.

As such, you can understand how virginity was more than just a state of being for me, it became my identity. I was prideful about my virtue. I was not one of those girls who did those types of things with boys who would later break their heart. I failed recess because I did not play when it came to this! My only kiss was a peck on the lips by a boy in the regional church meeting when I was 12 years old. Somehow his sister found out and told my brother who told me to tell my mother

Grace sees past your mistakes to your heart.

before she finds out some other way and it breaks her heart. It was just a peck on the lips! That may have sealed my fear of messing up in this area. Word travels fast!

Fast forward to me being 23 years old in a "relationship," if you want to call it that, with a far more experienced, worldly older guy. My first real kiss! It was a bit aggressive, way too much tongue…But, I liked it! Fast forward even further through the soon to follow break up and period of no communication to me being 25 years old. He was very successful and owned his own software development company. After visiting me in El Paso, he offered to pay for me to come to where

22

he was contracted to work. He was understanding enough to get me my own hotel room. But, that wasn't enough to stop what seemed like the inevitable.

Mind you, I had never consumed enough alcohol to really feel it besides maybe once as a law student during Texas Relays. He intentionally got me tipsy. I think you know where this is going. My inhibitions were down. And some things happened that were outside of my standard of behavior, although he kept his pants on. I would give you more details, but this is Fifty Shades of Grace, not Fifty Shades of Grey. LOL. All kidding aside, I was devastated. I knew that my behavior was not in line with the ideal standard and it caused me to question my very identity. Was I still a virgin? Even so, I was not as pure as I once was. The name Karen means pure. If I am not as pure as I should be, then who am I?

Add to that my closest friend at the time really condemned me and treated me like my behavior was detestable. How could I do such a thing? I went into a depression because I let myself down. I let God down. I let my parents down. I let my best friend down. I was a let down. Having defined myself by my "untouched" nature, I lost myself in my failure. Because I did not really understand grace, I felt as though it was a moment that changed everything for the worse. Life as I had once known it was over. After confessing to my pastors/parents, they assured me that I was still a virgin; but it took time to get my strength back.

Now that you probably think I'm a weirdo, let me explain myself. In my mind, I needed to be perfect for God. I was the example. If everyone else failed, I needed to succeed to prove that it was not impossible for God to keep you. I felt like that is what God was calling me to do and I was good at it! Then, I failed. #RealityCheck. I was not the pristine, untouched virginal young woman that I defined myself as. I had messed up in that highly emphasized area. So, who was I now?

Had I understood more than just the Christian religion, if I understood the gospel, it could have saved me from such devastation. All I knew was that God was calling me to holiness. I did not realize that my actions could never measure up. That is why God sent His son Jesus to die on the cross. Because He loved me so much and knew that I could never be righteous in my own power. By placing my faith in Him, His righteousness is counted as mine; my sins were crucified on the cross and buried with him in the tomb. Now, I am free to walk in the newness of life that

He gave me access to when He was raised from the dead. There is therefore now now condemnation to those who are in Christ. Romans 8:1.

Proverbs tells us that a righteous man falls seven times and seven times he rises again. Somehow I thought that I was never supposed to fall. If I fell, it was all over. But, that is not the process of righteousness. No baby learns to walk without scooting, crawling, falling and crying over and over again. We have patience for the process of learning to walk for the cutest human beings on the planet because we know that is what it takes. Yet, somehow we expect ourselves to walk by faith without stumbling or falling. If we are patient with our babies, how much more patience and grace is exhibited by the Almighty God when it comes to His children!

Without an understanding of God's wonderful grace, a desire to be righteous is simply a recipe for a dissatisfied soul full of anguish, pain and a combination vacillating between self-loathing and self-righteousness. Pardon my French, but it sucks! That is no way to live, no way to have joy, no way to access God's promise of a rich and satisfying life! It is hell on earth as you fear hell after earth. It is torture. Maybe you have suffered from some similar type of inner turmoil. Maybe it has made you consider giving up on this "Christian" life altogether because it just doesn't work in your own strength. I wrote this book just for you. It is time to give up toiling, sweating, white knuckling the discipline that it takes to be a Christian. It is time to instead discover the reality of Christ Jesus and the amazing grace that sets us free from the law of sin and death!

Perhaps you relate to the feeling of having disappointed yourself, but not the PG example I gave you. Let me assure you that I have done worse. MUCH WORSE. That was just an example. After all, my mother is going to read this. Suffice it to say that I know deep pain and disappointment from failing to meet the expectations I had for myself. I know what it feels like to be derailed from your dream life because you lost the battle with temptation and fell into a cycle of sin that made you question your very identity. I also know the pain and regret that comes from seeing someone succeed for God where I failed. However, allow me to offer a more extreme real-life example. Rahab was an entrepreneur, the likes of which many may turn up their nose. Her business was a hotel / brothel. The Bible describes her as a harlot, also known as a prostitute. But, Rahab had one thing going for her besides knowing how to shake her assets for cash.

She had heard of the children of Israel during their time after escaping from Egypt. She heard of their exploits, how God allowed them to walk through the Red Sea on dry land. She heard of their decimating other people groups in battle through the power of God. Faith comes by hearing. Rahab put her faith in God and helped the Hebrew spies when they came to scope out Jericho's defenses. Her belief in God was so profound that she betrayed her own people because she knew they would lose against God's people.

Because of her faith, she became an adopted part of the Hebrew family. You might assume that because of her past, she stayed single for the rest of her life. After all, who would want to marry someone who was had by so many? Your assumption would be incorrect. Not only did she marry; she had a son named Boaz. In the book of Ruth, Boaz symbolized a type of Christ. What's more, the scripture traces Christ's lineage and guess who you find? Rahab! With one decision to serve God and His people, she went from her sexuality being her largest claim to fame to becoming part of the lineage of Jesus Christ!!! She went from ho to holy. (Forgive me, I couldn't resist.)

Maybe you are broken. Maybe you have been used. Maybe you have been abused. Maybe you abused yourself because heretofore you did not recognize your worth and you sold your soul to meet your immediate needs. Maybe you have been categorized as the worst type of person who does the filthiest of things. Different sins may have different consequences. But, the state of sin encapsulates them all. Either you have been perfect in keeping every aspect of God's law or you have not. No matter your particular sin or weakness, there is nothing so bad, so filthy that it is beyond Christ's power to redeem you.

Consider this, if Mary, known for her virtue was the mother of Jesus Christ and Rahab was the mother of Boaz, who was an archetype of Christ in the old testament, then in heaven's record Rahab is in a class with and worthy of comparison to Mary! How can the righteousness of a prostitute be worthy of compare with that of a virgin? The same way that God can wipe your slate clear from all of your past, present and future sins! The answer is through faith! Our identity is not established by our past experiences; through faith our identity is found in Christ! That means that through faith you are the righteousness of God in Christ Jesus no matter what. It's not about your flaws. It is about Christ's perfection.

I love Christine Caine. Ok, so I don't really know Christine Caine personally. I am just a regular person and she is an all-star in the Kingdom of God. However, I have read her books and heard her preach. She is amazing! After being sexually abused by multiple men, multiple times a week for 12 long years, she discovered that she was, in fact, adopted. Not only did she have to get over the fact that she was abused, she had to deal with the fact that everything she thought she knew about her family was a lie. In trying to find out something about where she came from, she discovered her birth record. Not only did it become clear that her birth mother did not want anything to do with her, her birth certificate did not even have a name. She was abused, born unclaimed and unnamed. But, through the grace of Jesus Christ she overcame! She has written best-selling books, preaches internationally and founded the A21 Campaign which literally rescues people from sex slavery. I highly recommend you follow her ministry to learn more about her amazing grace-filled life. If she can be free from her past, and in turn living a life setting other captives free, imagine what God can do through you if you let go of your past and surrender to His love and purpose for you.

If you have been bound by your past for whatever the reason, it is freedom time! That is not encouragement to live your life your way without regard to God's guidelines. No way! That's not freedom. That is bondage to sin. True freedom comes when we receive righteousness (right standing with God) as a free grace gift through Christ. Now we stop working, striving and toiling to be righteous. You could never earn it! Now we walk in our identity in Christ that supersedes any mistakes or lapses in judgment. Even when we sin, our righteous identity does not change.

What did it take for you to have the color eyes you have? What did you have to do to get the skin you're in? What was the process for obtaining your parent's last name? How did you go about establishing your identity within your family structure? There was nothing you could do. All I had to do is be born and I was a Johnson just like that! I had my daddy's eyes, my mom's face, etc. just because I was born. Of course, I had to grow into the fullness of who I am, but I was a Johnson from day one. That is just how your righteousness is through Christ. You're fully righteous on day one, but you have to grow into the fullness of who you are. Let that sink in. From the day you accept Christ aka are born again, you are as forgiven as you ever will be. You are as righteous as you ever will become. You have the genetic traits of your Heavenly Father. You just need to grow in relationship with him and into the fullness of who you really are. Whatever that process of growth may be, it does not take away from your identity. You were born into it by faith!

1) Have you been striving in your own power to become who God wants you to be?

2) How has that been working for you? Have you failed yourself yet?

3) Are you ready to do things differently?

CHAPTER FOUR:

GRACE IS SUFFICIENT –
SAVED BY GRACE

If you would have asked the small child version of me what I wanted to be when I grew up, I would have answered, "A singer, a lawyer and a model." As I matriculated through high school and college my desire to be a famous singer/entertainer continued to grow. As a child, I wanted to be like Whitney Houston. As a young adult, Lauryn Hill was my prototype! Her music was culturally relevant, yet spiritual and full of biblical truths. And, she was an actress. That's what I wanted to do.

I wanted to follow the Queen Latifah/LL Cool J model and use music to positively influence people's lives and then spring board into acting. So by the time I graduated from law school, I did not want to be a lawyer. With my whole heart, I wanted to be discovered. I had an actual fear of being ordinary. I wanted to be known and influential. I still want to do something significant enough for NPR to at least mention my name when I pass away. My ambition and perhaps unrealistic expectation made my reality a real let down. I believe that God had a greater purpose and I am walking in it now. But, that did not stop the pain of disappointment from ringing out my heart like a wash rag during the season in which I had to relinquish my dreams of walking the red carpet.

You would not be able to tell by the fact that I am not currently practicing full time; however, I am licensed to practice law in Texas and California. Taking the Texas Bar Exam was the singular most difficult intellectual endeavor I ever attempted. I took it a couple of years after graduating law school when my music career failed to take off. For me, taking the bar was a certain sign of defeat. My dreams failed to come true and now I was relegated to living my life in an ordinary, unspectacular, hum drum existence. I know it's kind of weird. But, I had myself convinced that being a lawyer was a sign that I was a failure. So there was a painful type of stress in feeling like studying for the exam made me a failure.

Add to that the rigors of studying for a two-and-a-half-day exam, one of the most difficult bar exams in the country. There is one day of just multiple choice questions – a full day! But, these aren't the sort of multiple choice questions that gave you a sigh of relief during your high school pop quiz days. I wish. There could be an entire page of small-lettered reading followed by three or four complex multiple choice questions related to the passage. Furthermore, this was a timed exam. You had to answer the questions before the clock ran out. I think that left around two minutes per question. Then there were the essays, the short answer, and the mock practice where you were put in an imaginary state with imaginary statutes and imaginary precedent, given imaginary facts and told to draft a sound legal document. Yikes!!!

Needless to say, studying for the Texas Bar Exam sucked. (Pardon my French.) This test would determine whether or not the student loans (which I'm still paying) were a wasted investment, whether my life was poured down the drain when I attended law school. This one exam was the measurement of my worth in the legal profession. My face was broken out in pimples, which inevitably left long-lasting dark marks from hyper pigmentation. My hair actually started coming out! I was completely and totally stressed the _____ out! Part of the reason it was so stressful was the underlying question of whether or not I would succeed. Am I studying enough? Am I working hard enough? Ultimately, the real question was am I enough?

For those who struggle with the issue, part of what fuels our perfectionism is fear that who we are at the moment is not enough. Not enough to be successful. Not enough to deserve love. Not enough to make it. It is the fear that unless we try harder, get better, go faster and stronger we will not be worthy of love and acceptance. We all need love and acceptance on a deep, primal level. So, as a part of our survival instinct, we strive for perfection to attain love and acceptance we so desperately need.

Maybe you have never thought of it that way before, but right now internally, your spirit is giving that truth a head nod. At the core of our addiction to pursuing perfect, is the fear that who we are in our imperfection is not enough. It is fear that our flaws, failures and/or lack of sufficient accomplishment renders us worth less. Thus, who we are is not valuable enough to exchange for what we need to survive. That reasoning would make sense if it were all dependent on us. However, it is not all dependent on us. The grace of God bridges the gap between our inadequacy and true perfection which is only found in Christ.

In 2 Corinthians 12:7-10 New King James Version, Paul writes:

And lest I should be exalted above measure by the abundance of the revelations, a thorn in the flesh was given to me, a messenger of Satan to buffet me, lest I be exalted above measure. Concerning this thing I pleaded with the Lord three times that it might depart from me. And He said to me, "My grace is sufficient for you, for My strength is made perfect in weakness." Therefore most gladly I will rather boast in my infirmities, that the power of Christ may rest upon me. Therefore I take pleasure in infirmities, in reproaches, in needs, in persecutions, in distresses, for Christ's sake. For when I am weak, then I am strong.

Some say that the word thorn would better be translated as a stake, you know the significantly larger wooden weapon needed to pierce the heart in order to kill the vampire according to the movies. Think of a rose. A thorn may be the length of your pinky nail, but thinner. If you Google stake, this is the definition you get: *a strong wooden or metal post with a point at one end, driven into the ground to support a tree, form part of a fence, act as a boundary mark, etc.* See the difference? Imagine the distinction between having a rose's thorn in your flesh (ouch…annoying) and a stake large enough to support a tree (someone call 911…I might die)! I don't claim to know what type of pain Paul endured because of this stake that pierced his flesh, be it physical or psychological. Some suggest it

…there is nothing so bad, so filthy that it is beyond Christ's power to redeem you.

was some sort of physical ailment that was apparent to his contemporary audience thus it wouldn't need to be spelled out because it was obvious to his readers. Others opine that it was a temptation of sorts or something else mental like anxiety or depression.

Whatever it was, it was something that impeded Paul's ability to be perfect. It was something hellish, something that didn't seem like it belonged with a man who received revelations from God. It didn't fit into Paul's image as "the Apostle." It was a painful reality that was off-brand. It was something that he likely feared would hinder him from accomplishing his purpose. It was something that Paul never posted on Instagram or tweeted about. He always took his selfies at an angle that minimized whatever this thing was. It was something that brought shame and humiliation to the deepest parts of his soul.

This thorn was something that was severe enough to act as a counter weight to Paul's numerous revelations from God. This imperfection kept him down to earth despite the elation he experienced every time he obtained heavenly insight. That means that whatever it was, it had to be — heavy. Overall, Paul seems like a pretty confident, extremely accomplished man. But, this stake in his flesh was painful enough to bring out the beggar in him. "Please God! Remove this stake from my flesh! Please! Please!"

Despite all of your success and the projected confidence that can be seen on the surface of your life, is there something that brings out the beggar in you? "Please God! Take away my _____." Fill in the blank with whatever disappointment brings you to your knees. Please God! Take away my lustful desire for pornography. Please God! Take away the pain from my divorce. Please God! Rescue my adult child from addiction. Please God! Heal my heart from the countless wounds of rejection. Please God! . . .

Paul described the main weighty, painful, shameful thing that he wished he could change about his life as a stake in his flesh. That means whatever it was, it was not going away. It was something deeply embedded into the nature of his being. It was not getting any better. Paul showed no signs of progress concerning this thing. The prognosis was bleak. He went to the ER, described the pain to the doctor and the doctor replied, "I don't need an X-Ray. It's obvious there is a stake in your flesh. But, there's nothing we can do to help. You're just going to have to live with it." Wait. What!?!

He cried out to God not once, not twice, but three times. "Please! Please! Please!" like James Brown without background singers. And it is not that God did not hear him. We know God heard him because He responded. But, what do you do when God's response is not in line with what you hoped to hear? "My Grace is sufficient

31

for you, for my strength is made perfect in weakness." That is definitely not what you would expect as the testimony from a man of such great faith and power. No such weakness could be known by God and left alone for His glory. That just doesn't happen. God does not operate like that. Or does He?

Through this excruciating issue, Paul discovered that the closest he will ever come to perfection is weakness. God's strength is made perfect in weakness. So he was strongest in the places where he was weak because the strength that manifested during those times was not his own. That strength came from God!

But, what if Paul's pursuit of perfection made him deny his weakness. What if he refused to admit any lack of strength within himself? What if Paul was so busy trying to fix himself that he never allowed his spirit to be enraptured with revelation? You know how we do. "God I will serve you when I have fixed myself." "I can't pray for anybody right now; I've got too many issues." "When this stake issue gets cleared up and I get my life together, then I will spread the gospel, start my business, adopt a child. . .do whatever it is God told me to do."

If Paul waited until he was perfect, he never would have impacted the ancient world and subsequently the modern world with the Gospel of Jesus Christ. Half of the New Testament would have never been written. Paul had to recognize that it was not about him. It wasn't about his imperfections; it was about God's perfection. It wasn't about his weakness; it was about God's strength. Paul had to learn to be a blessing despite his brokenness.

Just like Paul, we have to get the lesson. It's not about you! It is not about your wonderfulness or your weakness. It is about God's strength in you. You have to walk in purpose despite your pain. **You can win even with your weakness if you build even while you're broken.**

How do you do this? By recognizing that God's Grace is sufficient. Merriam-Webster defines sufficient as *having or providing as much as is needed*. Whatever the situation, His Grace is all you need! You are worthy in His Grace. You are strong in His Grace. You are successful in His Grace. You are effective in His Grace. You are loved in His Grace. You are accepted in His Grace. You are fearless in His Grace.

God's Grace is as much as you need. The bigger the need, the bigger His Grace will show up to meet it! Your survival is not dependent on your ability to measure up. Your survival is secure in His Grace! There is no need to fear. No need to chase perfection, lest you die with your needs unmet. God's Grace is enough!

Several years after I passed the Texas Bar, I found myself in a position to take the California Bar Exam. This time, I was determined not to allow the experience to be as painful. I refused to allow myself to be as stressed. I would simply do the work and trust that it would be sufficient for me to pass. This time, I was armed with the knowledge that I had already passed one of the most difficult bar exams in the country and I was already a lawyer. Because of that victory, I knew that I was enough. All I had to do was focus my energy towards enduring the process.

The second time around I was not working to prove that I had what it took. I knew that I had the requisite intelligence and test-taking skills. All I had to do is demonstrate it on the exam. When I took the Texas Bar, I was working to prove I was enough. When I took the California Bar, I was working from the place of already being enough. That subtle articulation equates to a monumental shift in thinking and my experience. Make no mistake, studying for the bar was still a lot of discipline and hard work. However, I was so much less stressed the second time around. I did not have the added pressure of trying to establish my identity and worthiness in the exam. After all, it was just a test.

Hey you! Yeah, you! Stop stressing out! The challenge that you are facing is only a test. The issue that you are struggling with does not determine your identity or your worth. It is just an opportunity to demonstrate the victory that you already have attained in Christ. You've got what it takes to succeed. Greater is He that is in you than he that is in the world. You've got the grace of God in your corner. You may need to retreat in His presence in-between rounds to catch your breath, let him coach you and regain your strength. But, make no mistake about it, your grace trainer is shouting for you to get back in the ring and fight until you win!

If God's grace is enough, you do not have to work for fulfillment; you can work from fulfillment. You do not have to work for worthiness; you can work from a state of worthiness. Whatever you accomplish externally, is merely an outward manifestation of the seed that already lies within. You have nothing to prove! You are already accepted in the beloved. Ephesians 1:6. You are already enough in

Christ. You don't have to earn it. Just believe it; receive it; and walk in it.

Before you get out of bed in the morning, you are enough. Before you scratch the first thing off of your to-do list for the day, you are enough. Before you are boo'd up (an African American colloquialism meaning in a romantic relationship), you are enough. Before your children make the honor roll, you are enough. Before you own your home, you are enough. Before you make partner, you are enough. You will accomplish what you accomplish because you have what it takes. It is out of the reservoir of who you are that you will water the seed of your achievements. It is out of your being that you will do, not the other way around. It is never the other way around. You are already enough.

1) Is there an area in your life that brings out the beggar in you?

2) Is there something beyond your control in your life that makes you feel as though it will inhibit your success?

3) Do you realize that you can win even with your weakness? Make a decision not to let anything stop you from obtaining God's best for your life.

CHAPTER FIVE:

CONFESSION IS GOOD FOR THE SOUL

H ave you ever had a secret? I'm not talking about a surprise party that you are trying to keep under wraps so you tell a little white lie to throw the birthday girl off the trail. I am asking if you have ever been burdened by something in your past that brought a sense of shame and insecurity. Have you ever felt as though there was something about you that made you unworthy of love? Something that if known would ensure you would not find a place of belonging? I have.

Please forgive my lack of candor concerning the specifics like the unnamed stake in Paul's flesh. I am referring to something the enemy of my soul tried to use in order to make me feel ruined, like I was no longer fit for service. The thing that made me feel disqualified from fulfilling my divine destiny. It's something that shook me to my core. I wondered who I was because of it. I wondered if I could ever really recover from it.

I have a lot of things going for me. But, my fear told me that this thing made me unlovable. The dark whisper in my soul said that it would cause my love to be recalled like a faulty airbag on an otherwise attractive model, leading to instant buyer's remorse. Yet, I had to take full responsibility. There was no one to blame, but me. It was not the sort of thing that would likely even risk exposure from those superficial relationships we all have in our lives. My concern was that it would prevent me from having a deep connection with someone. It caused me to question the likelihood of finding someone who could know everything about me and still love me and still choose me. Someone reading this relates to what I am saying.

Then, I met Antoine, the man who would ultimately change my name. This guy was serious! I kid you not. On our very first date he asked about my credit score! He even asked about whether I had any major health issues that he should know about. SMH I still can't believe his boldness. He later told me that before we met he saw me on stage at church. He assumed I was taken. But, he said to himself in his New York slang kind of way, "If I ever got a chance with her, I would marry her." I knew that he liked what he saw from afar. But, he couldn't see my secret.

Even in the beginning, Antoine was amazing. My skin had broken out terribly! There were dark marks where pimples had been. I did not feel the most attractive. But, he insisted on seeing me without my make up and still called me beautiful. This man would pop my pimples with glee! He offered to help me take the extensions out of my hair when it was time to take my hair down. And he subsequently sat there with a rat-tail comb and actually did it! Who does that!?! I had never met anyone like him. Talks of marriage came up, but I absolutely could not let it get that far with this secret weighing on me. Yet, telling him this could ruin everything!

I knew this would be the one thing that could make him change his mind. It would make or break the relationship. But, I had to tell him. Am I the only one who finds it easier to put really difficult things in writing? I texted, "I need to tell you something." Moments later, he called me. My heart felt like an earthquake in my chest. Despite the looming internal natural disaster, I had to say it. I gathered all of the courage I could and just said it. My confession was met with silence.

I held my breath as I hoped that he would still want me. Then, Antoine said something that was even more amazing than my highest hopes for this moment of transparency. He said, "You telling me that makes me love you even more." OMG! Even as I write this tears are coming to my eyes to think that someone can love me the way that he does. His love and acceptance goes beyond my imagination! I knew then he was the one. That sealed it for me.

If we confess our sins, He is faithful and just to forgive us our sins and to
cleanse us from all unrighteousness.
1 John 1:9 NKJV

You don't have to be burdened by anything in your past or anything in your present. God already knows everything about you. Yet, He loves you with a perfect love that is beyond all comprehension. You can confess whatever secret has been weighing you down. He knows it anyway! He loves you anyway! Why suffer from the depression that comes from bearing the weight of that thing, whatever it is on your shoulders? If you confess, if you repent, God's response is as predictable as the sun rising in the east.

He won't ridicule you. He won't belittle you. He won't put you on blast and humiliate you for the world to see. If you confess/repent of your sins, He will forgive you and cleanse you every time! I have an inkling He has already forgiven you, but in order for you to access the forgiveness and experience the relief that comes from knowing you are in right standing with him, you must confess/repent. Because God already loves you perfectly So He cannot say that He loves you even more because you told him. But, you will feel His love cascade over your being even more without the secret acting as an umbrella, shielding the rain of His love from your soul.

God is a gentleman. He will not force you. You have to give him permission to let the love in. When you confess, you do just that. His perfect love casts out fear. You can go from being burdened to just being blessed. The cleansing water of His forgiveness will wash away any doubt that you are loved by and accepted in him. Why go another day carrying the weight of your secret when His grace is enough?

1) Is there an unconfessed area in your life that is preventing you from receiving God's love?

2) If you knew beyond a shadow of a doubt that if you confessed that thing, God would forgive you and cleanse you, would you confess it?

3) Sometimes you just need to act in faith even before your mind can comprehend a thing. Take a moment now to tell God the thing you were afraid to talk about and receive His love, His forgiveness, and His cleansing that is waiting for you.

* My mom wanted me to add this "important caution."

Her words:
Confess your sins to each other and pray for each other so that you may be healed. The earnest prayer of a righteous person has great power and produces wonderful results. James 5:16 (NLT) *"You must be aware not everyone is spiritual enough to receive your confession. Religious, legalistic people who are still too ignorant of their own sin don't qualify to restore you."* In other words, don't tell your business to just anybody. You will find telling some people is a mistake because they aren't mature enough to handle it. As I said in Grace Reflection Three above, tell God!

CHAPTER SIX:

THE F WORD

My mother seems as if she was born the 1st Lady of a church, like her first words were quotations from the King James Version of the Bible. I'm so serious! She is so dignified and gracious, like she is Christian royalty. I have a lot in common with my momma. But, they don't make them like her anymore! God broke that first lady mold after she popped out of it.

I'm a little more rebellious. I remember venting about something and I was like, "F that!" She gasped, dramatically, holding her mouth agape! "Don't say that! Do you know what that stands for?" And I said, "F? It's just a letter." Of course I knew better. But, I could not let her have the pleasure! I'm not talking about that F word here. But, the word I'm talking about can sometimes be met with even more incredulity. This F Word is FORGIVENESS.

Forgiveness can be a very hard pill to swallow because sometimes it feels as if we are saying that the wrong others have done to us is ok. That is not what it is at all. But, that is what it can feel like. It's as though we're giving a pass to someone to do it again. But, that's not it either. The truth is forgiveness is one of the greatest gifts you can give yourself, despite how it may seem.

As I mentioned before, it was my dream since childhood to be a famous singer. It was kind of weird because my singing gift was not the most affirmed growing up. I figured since I couldn't sing well enough, I would rap. Then, sophomore year of college Lauryn Hill dropped her Miseducation album and I decided I would sing and rap! You get the idea. It was my long-held dream.

I thought Amy (the name has been changed as to not put her business in the streets) was my best friend. I met her Sophomore year at the church I attended while in college. She was an incoming freshman at the same school. She latched on to me right away. I gave her rides to church. For some reason, I had an extra bed in my dorm room and she would spend the night so frequently, I had to kindly invite her to go to her freshman dorm. I'm an extrovert, but I still need my space.

She was a local and had deep roots in the area. Her mom was an elder at the church and it made me feel even more connected. We had so much in common as PKs. We performed spoken word and rapped at the church together. Amy was super smart and we both wanted to do something great in the earth. We would talk for hours on the phone even over summer break as teenage girls tend to do. God only knows how many hours were spent between the two of us.

Then, tragedy struck. Second semester, senior year, Amy got the devastating news that her mom had cancer and it didn't look good. Her mom was a single parent and a powerful force not only in her life, but in the church and the community at large. I remember skipping all of my classes that day, yet having the consciousness to go to my professors and telling them what was up. I am not sure why I even did that. I was such a nerd! I don't even remember where we went, but I cannot forget how she cried and I held her hand. It was as though we knew things would not be ok.

That summer my mother even opened up our home to her mother, a perfect stranger as she sought alternative treatment in Mexico. I remember her mom's heart-wrenching, shrill cries in the middle of the night when she was just trying to make it to the restroom a few feet outside the guest room, but just could not do it because of the pain in her body. Amy had returned home to set up their home like a hospital to care for her mom with all that she had.

That fall I began law school at The University of Texas School of Law. Throughout the semester, night after night after night and day after day I took calls from Amy where she would be crying and venting and frustrated and exhausted. I was not there, but I definitely carried the weight of her condition. Combined with the stress of trying to acclimate to the beast that is law school, it was more than I felt like I could handle. I remember letting her know at one point, "You can't only call me crying…" I needed a break of some kind myself. I was there for her the best way I could be.

Then, the unthinkable happened. I got the call that her mother had transitioned. I had the same sick feeling in my core, just deeper and more intense. Just before my first set of law school finals, I was on a plane headed back to be there for my friend. I rode in the limo with the family, sat on the front row with the family and held her hand. Grief.

As a community leader, Amy's mom was well connected. After her passing, she offered to use her mother's connections to help me live my dream. She wanted to manage my budding music career. Why would I say no? What is better than having your best friend help you to make your dreams come true? How much time and money did I spend putting together press packs, and burning CDs, and shipping it to the east coast so she could work on our big break!?

God's Grace is as much as you need.

By the summer after law school graduation, she had managed to get an A&R of a major label to present my demo to a big time record exec. I was elated and decided not to take the bar with my peers. I was going to live my dreams instead! That opportunity came and went as did countless others. I thought it was par for the course, a thousand No's to get to the one Yes. Story after story, detailed meetings with names you might recognize were relayed to me long distance, and over a year passed with nothing. That's why I was so disappointed when I had to take the bar exam.

I started working as an Assistant District Attorney. It was cool. However, in my mind it was only temporary because I was still awaiting my big break. Finally, it seemed like she had landed the most significant opportunity yet. Amy had met the manager / label co-owner with an artist who had the hottest song of the summer! "Pack your bags!" she said, "Any day now, you will be getting a call from me to fly to NY to meet them."

One week passed. "They had to go to Europe so it can't be this week." Another week passed. "They're on tour, but I've already spoken with the marketing director and they're trying to figure out how to market you." Another week. "They are trying to figure out whether you will be on their imprint or the major label above them, which is a better fit." Finally, after years of this type of torment in a very casual conversation with my parents, they said, "Take everything she [Amy] says with a grain of salt. She has been saying all of these things and nothing has ever happened."

That is when it hit me. I had no proof whatsoever that any of her stories were true. None! Sometimes I would mistakenly leave my phone during my work day at the DA and I would come home to a bunch of missed calls. "Where were you?" Amy would say. "I had _____ on the line to talk to you, but you didn't pick up." The person was always on the line, but I never once spoke to anyone…ever. Oh no! Could it be what I think it is? Had she been lying to me for years while I made real life decisions based on the information she was feeding me about my future!?! Could it be?

The one piece of information I had was this particular manager's number. Driving to choir rehearsal one night soon after the conversation with my parents, I decided to use it. Ring. Ring. He picks up the phone, "Hello." "Yes this is Solre (my stage name)." "Who?" "Solre. I think Amy gave you my music." "Oh yeah. What's up…" I already knew from his very chilly response that everything she had said about them being on the verge of signing me to a deal with their record label was a lie. I knew instantly that if the most real, closest opportunity I had ever gotten through her was not real, then none of the other things she had ever said were real.

It was all a lie. Years of my life gone. Opportunities to go other directions and pursue other things. Gone! My hopes and dreams. All Gone! I spoke with Amy about it and she never owned up to it. I told her that Saturday that my parents thought she was lying and I thought she was lying. If she was lying, she couldn't be my manager or my friend. She assured me she wasn't. Early Sunday morning I got an ice cold email from Amy saying she had contacted everyone and put everything on hold because I believed she was a pathological liar. She didn't even realize that if she could contact everyone in an afternoon, it was only confirmation of the fact that she had no one to contact.

It was all over. I did not speak to her after that. I don't know that I can put into words the level of deep disappointment that I endured. How could I have believed her! How could I be such a fool! Why would she lie like that for all that time!?! It's not like I was paying her money or something. It just didn't make sense. But, it was what it was. I had to keep going to work and doing a good job. Kept serving in the church like nothing had happened. All the while I was dying inside of the betrayal I had suffered.

This was the first time in my life I had visions of violence. Seriously! I literally could see myself grabbing her by the neck and squeezing with all my might. "It is a good thing she is on the east coast and I am in El Paso, TX," I thought. I was so angry! If I saw her, we would fight. It would be the first real physical altercation of my life! It was going to be Love and Hip Hop before such a thing existed! I saw it so vividly!

About a year later she texted me from a strange number. I will spare you the details, but she did not apologize. Yet, I felt within my heart that the Holy Spirit was impressing upon me to tell her that she was forgiven. What!?! I had a WWE wrestling match in my soul. I did not want to do that. Tell her she's forgiven?!? The F Word!?! After all, that she put me through and all I ever was was good to her? Nope! Nuh-uh. I don't think so.

"Tell her she is forgiven." But, wait, I don't want to lie. Is she forgiven? Step 1: If I saw her, would I still want to choke her!?!… Back and forth. Finally, I heard within, "Tell her she is forgiven as though you are speaking for me." In other words, it's not about you, do what I said. I did not want to. But, I really love God and I want him to be pleased with me. So I grabbed my phone, typed out, "You are forgiven" even though she never apologized. I pushed send and I knew that I had done what God wanted me to do. Moments later Amy launched right back into, "Well I do have some contacts …" "I don't want your contacts." SMH

The F word is one of the most powerful words in the heart of humanity. Forgiveness is a profound concept that challenges us to ascend to god-like character. "To err is human; to forgive is divine." It really is something that calls upon the highest level of our nature to do. Yet, we have the power to do it. This next passage from Matthew 18:21-35 in the New Living Translation is a little lengthy, but powerful and worth our attention:

21 Then Peter came to him and asked, "Lord, how often should I forgive someone who sins against me? Seven times?"

22 "No, not seven times," Jesus replied, "but seventy times seven!

23 "Therefore, the Kingdom of Heaven can be compared to a king who decided to bring his accounts up to date with servants who had borrowed money from him. 24 In the process, one of his debtors was brought in who owed him millions of dollars.

25 He couldn't pay, so his master ordered that he be sold—along with his wife, his children, and everything he owned—to pay the debt.

26 "But the man fell down before his master and begged him, 'Please, be patient with me, and I will pay it all.' 27 Then his master was filled with pity for him, and he released him and forgave his debt.

28 "But when the man left the king, he went to a fellow servant who owed him a few thousand dollars. He grabbed him by the throat and demanded instant payment.

29 "His fellow servant fell down before him and begged for a little more time. 'Be patient with me, and I will pay it,' he pleaded. 30 But his creditor wouldn't wait. He had the man arrested and put in prison until the debt could be paid in full.

31 "When some of the other servants saw this, they were very upset. They went to the king and told him everything that had happened. 32 Then the king called in the man he had forgiven and said, 'You evil servant! I forgave you that tremendous debt because you pleaded with me. 33 Shouldn't you have mercy on your fellow servant, just as I had mercy on you?' 34 Then the angry king sent the man to prison to be tortured until he had paid his entire debt.

35 "That's what my heavenly Father will do to you if you refuse to forgive your brothers and sisters from your heart."

There is so much in this passage. But, for brevity's sake let's cut to the chase. A major part of the grace gift granted to us by our heavenly Father is forgiveness for ALL of our sin. Part of our

You don't have to be burdened by anything in your past or anything in your present.

ability to receive His forgiveness rests upon our ability to give it. I have heard that the difference between the Dead Sea and the Red Sea is the Red Sea is flowing water full of life while the Dead Sea is stagnant because the water the comes in does not flow out. The water of God's forgiveness must flow through you to flow to you. Otherwise, you will be dead inside.

Unforgiveness leads to bondage and torture. You cannot stand guard and hold someone hostage to their past actions without holding yourself hostage at the same time. Forgiveness sets you free. Forgiveness is how you take your power back from the person that hurt you. It disempowers the offender and empowers the one who forgives.

In this scripture, the Greek word used for forgiveness is aphiēmi, which means to release from the consequences that might otherwise reasonably have accrued to the debt or misdeed. Forgiveness means writing off what is owed to you in order to bring your life into balance. One of my least favorite college courses was accounting. You have the ledger where the financial record is kept and when done correctly and your accounts receivable is up to date, both sides of the ledger are supposed to be equal. But, what if there is a deficit? What if someone owes you money, like the example in scripture. If someone has taken something from you and not paid you back, that leads to an imbalance on your ledger.

That imbalance can follow you year after year after year as you keep carrying over the debt, holding on to what someone owes you. For those of you who like me are not accountants, you realize how unnerving this imbalance can be. What if you could start over with a clean slate and a perfect balance? You can. That is what forgiveness does. It writes off the debt so that the ledger of your life can come back into balance. As long as you hold the person to their debt, you suffer. When you let them go, you set yourself free! It is an amazing thing.

Furthermore, it is impossible to receive forgiveness if you do not give it. There's just something about it. The way you judge others is a reflection of how you already judge yourself. Those who freely forgive freely receive forgiveness and those who don't don't. I could list several more scriptures to prove my point. But, this is really not about overwhelming you with information. I want to empower you to live your best life. Rest assured, holding on to unforgiveness will get in the way of that every single time.

If you came from a background of sexual, physical or emotional abuse or you suffered a betrayal that makes mine look like child's play, you may not relate to my personal example. Perhaps you would benefit from Joyce Meyers' testimony of coming to forgive and become the caretaker of the father that raped her for years in her youth. It takes a tremendous amount of grace. But, God has already supplied you with the sufficient amount of grace for you to walk in forgiveness and live free from further victimization. Do not hold yourself hostage, shackled to someone else's wrong. Do not forsake your future because you are imprisoned by your past. Forgiveness sets you free.

—— GRACE REFLECTIONS ————————————————————

1) Is there someone you need to forgive?

2) Have you noticed that holding that person hostage has also kept you in bondage?

3) It is time to forgive. It is not a feeling; it is a decision. Make the choice to forgive and your feelings will follow.

CHAPTER SEVEN:

F YOURSELF

Have you ever had a deep regret? Something that caused shame and condemnation every time you think about it? One of those things that you feel as though if you had done differently your whole life would be better? Something for which you carry guilt like it is the honorable thing to do, self-discipline for the mistake that you cannot undo? I felt so stupid for believing Amy. I was such a fool! How could I let myself be strung along for all of those years! I had to take responsibility for letting myself be lied to. Now the prime years for the pursuit of my dreams had passed and there was nothing I could do to get it back.

Maybe there is something in your life that you wish you could get back. It could be something that seems way bigger than what I am talking about. It could be that you wronged someone else in some irreparable way. Perhaps you got caught up in something that you are so ashamed of that it seems to sit on your chest and take your breath away. Drug addiction. Reckless sexual activity that has negatively impacted both your body and your mind. Racism. Abortion. Gang affiliation. Fraud. Divorce. Scandal. Maybe it is not someone else you need to forgive. Perhaps you need to forgive yourself.

There is that F word again! There are times in life where it is easier to forgive someone else than to forgive yourself. You may even be saying to yourself, I know God forgives me, but this guilt and shame is the consequence of my sin so it's just something I will have to deal with for the rest of my life. Guilt and shame is not the cross that you must bear. No! Jesus bore all of your shame and guilt, all of your regret for every sin on the cross. Romans 8:1 lets us know that there is now no condemnation to those who belong to Christ. The condemnation should not exist in your now. The shame has no place in the now. The guilt has no place in now. That was then, this is now.

Stop condemning yourself now. Just quit it! You are not doing yourself, God or anyone else a favor to continuously punish yourself with negative self-talk and your allegiance to guilt and shame. That is not your responsibility. It is your responsibility to receive the grace and forgiveness paid for at the cross by Christ himself. How can you be held to a debt that has already been paid? If you were at a restaurant, ready to leave and you discovered your bill was paid in full, gratuity and all, would you insist on paying again?

"I'd like the bill please." "It has already been taken care of." "Taken care of? But, I didn't pay for it." "Someone else paid your bill for you." "I didn't ask them to do that. Bring me my bill anyway." "Your bill no longer exists. It has been paid in full." "I insist! I must pay for my meal." That is ridiculous behavior. When the bill is paid, you say thank you and keep your money.

Your debt has been paid. There is no point in spending your life trying to pay something that has already been eradicated. Furthermore, it is impossible for you to ever pay for your sins or earn your own redemption. This is one of those things that goes beyond what money can buy, beyond your ability to earn. You need a patron to pave the way, to grant forgiveness out of his own loving kindness. Guess what! That is exactly what you have in the grace gift of Jesus Christ. Jesus paid the ultimate price so that you can live forgiven for all of your sins, past, present and future.

Redemption is all about an exchange. God exchanged the precious life of His only begotten son for the capital punishment we deserved due to our sin. Now we get everlasting life because of Christ's righteousness. Forgiveness is available to you. But, you must accept the grace gift and show your gratitude by applying it to the areas in your life that need healing. You could not do it on your own no matter how hard you tried. So you might as well give it up to God. You could never do enough or be enough to make up for the past

Jesus is enough. There is no need for another sacrifice! Stop crucifying yourself over your past. Stop trying to suicide bomb your way into heaven, blowing away

50

your life with explosions of hopelessness and regret. It is impossible to do that without the people closest to you suffering too. Maybe you have even disqualified yourself from your God-given dream because you feel like you do not deserve it because of your past mistakes. Do you realize that God knew you before you were formed in your mother's womb? He knows your thoughts before you think them. Of course, He knows your mistakes before you make them. Yet, the all-knowing God has a calling on your life, a purpose for you to fulfill.

If God made you and He made your purpose, then doesn't it stand to reason that He made you with your purpose in mind? Every strength, every weakness, every proclivity, every aspect of your being was taken into consideration when God placed that purpose in your heart. He did not call you before you messed up and then change His mind. He called you from eternity, seeing and knowing all you would ever do before you were even born. Romans 11:29 says God's gifts and His call are irrevocable. He will never change His mind about you!

Lest you feel like your sin is beyond God's glorious grace, let me remind you of some of the heroes that we herald in the Bible:

Abraham – A Liar and Doubter of God

Jacob – A Pretender/Guilty of Fraud

Moses – A Murderer

David – A Murderer and Adulterer

Paul – A Terrorist who supported the killing of early Christians.

Need I go on? The fact that you have a messed up past puts you in the perfect place for God's grace to redeem you.

You are here for a reason. Do not let your past rob you of your potential. Not only has God the father given you the gift of grace, He has also given the world a gift through you. Humanity is awaiting the healing, the solution that only your fulfillment of purpose can bring. Do not rob the world of the gift that is you because of guilt and condemnation. Live like you are grateful for being forgiven.

The only way to do that is to let go of your past and embrace your future.

No, dear brothers and sisters, I have not achieved it, but I focus on this one thing: Forgetting the past and looking forward to what lies ahead, I press on to reach the end of the race and receive the heavenly prize for which God, through Christ Jesus, is calling us. Philippians 3:13-14 (NLT)

This was Paul's secret. No matter what, has happened, just keep pressing forward. Just like when you're driving a car, you tend to steer in the direction that you're looking. So Paul's secret was to look forward and press forward. Now your past may be haunting you. You don't need to call Ghost Busters. You need to forget it. Forget the past. Look forward. Press forward. Repeat every morning and throughout the day as necessary.

1) Do you have any regrets from your past that still bring you pain?

2) Is it possible that the reason it still hurts is because you need to forgive yourself?

3) It is time to forgive yourself. Forget the past. Look forward. And, press forward.

CHAPTER EIGHT:

PERFECTION IS AN URBAN LEGEND

An urban legend is often a somewhat bizarre story that is shared among modern city dwellers. The one that comes to mind is the man on a business trip that woke up in a tub full of ice in a strange motel room in the middle of nowhere to find a note that said his kidneys had been stolen and he needs to call 911. Have you heard that one? It is an urban legend because no matter how many times it is told, it still is not true. Unlike how Black folks have been saying there's vitamin C in Kool-Aid for so long that they finally put a teeny smidgen of vitamin C in there. Am I the only one who notices these things? But, I digress :) There is no such thing as a crime in which people's organs are stolen without their knowledge and they end up in a bathtub full of ice, at least not in the USA. Likewise, there is no such thing as perfect, at least not in the urban legend kind of way that we tend to see that word.

Webster's primary definition for perfect is exactly the urban legend kind of concept that I'm talking about: "having no mistakes or flaws." I believe it was Tal Ben-Shahar, one of Harvard's premier experts on happiness aka positive psychology, who broke it down this way: A bowler can potentially bowl a perfect game. Likewise, a golfer can golf a perfect game. These are quantifiable measures of perfection. However, even the greatest bowler or golfer in the history of the sport do not perform perfectly on a regular or semi-regular basis. Even to the best there ever was, a perfect round is an anomaly. Now try to apply that principle to life.

Maybe it is not someone else you need to forgive. Perhaps you need to forgive yourself.

How do you measure being a perfect mom? What does being a perfect son look like? What is the perfect career? The perfect life? How can you possibly attain something that cannot even be defined or quantified? If you were to

54

attain it, how would you even know it? It's like chasing the pot of gold at the end of the rainbow. The catch is you never find the end of the rainbow. You can run towards it with all of the might you possess. However, the moment you arrive to the place you think the rainbow ends you discover that you can no longer see the rainbow, you lose your frame of reference to what it was you were even chasing after.

Chasing perfection in the name of the pursuit of happiness is the national sport. But, how do you know when you've arrived? What measuring system are you using as a reference. Is it about keeping up with the Joneses? Giving as much as Mother Theresa? Getting a holiday named after you like Dr. Martin Luther the King? (Yes, I did mean "the King" as a Coming to America reference.) What is the measure of this legendary mistake-less, flawless life?

What in this life has no mistakes or flaws? Somebody tell me please. Oh, I know. Something that is synthetic, fake, manufactured. That double knit polyester suit from 1975 may seem perfect because the material was a man-made invention. But, anything that is natural has flaws. Perhaps you've seen the labels on clothes made of silk or some other delicate fabric. They say something like, "The inconsistency in this fabric is not a flaw; it is a natural characteristic of its beauty and part of its design."

If you came with a tag, it would say something similar. "The idiosyncrasies, insecurities and inadequacy in this person are not disqualifying traits; they are characteristics of her uniqueness and are necessary to demonstrate the glory of the Creator." We have this glory in earthen vessels so that it is obviously God and not us! 2 Corinthians 4:7 (KYDV Karen Yvonne Dykes Version) Hallelujah!

You are the Divine Designer's original. The things that you may perceive as weaknesses are the very things that distinguish you from the pack. God knew you before you were formed in the womb and while still in the hidden shadows of your mother's belly, He set you apart for His purpose. You are divinely designed for that which you are assigned! Fortunately, the pre-requisite for your fulfillment of purpose is not perfection. So do yourself a favor and stop believing that lie!

Forgiveness sets you free.

The imagination is a powerful thing. Remember being a child and seeing a shadow cast at bedtime from a night

FIFTY SHADES OF GRACE

light or the light from the hallway? In no time, you could transform the shapeless figure into your worst nightmare. Lurking in the shadows was Freddie Krueger or Jason or a random clown or whatever made your heart beat like you were about to have to fight for your life! A monster is chasing you; that is a scary thought.

As we get older, we start to create the idea of perfection out of the incomplete, one dimensional images we see in the magazines, on TV, Instagram, Facebook, Twitter, etc. Everyone and everything seems so bright as you scroll down your timeline. Everyone and everything is in just the right light, at the right angle, capturing the moments and subjects masterfully. It is out of this false light that we construct the monster of perfection. Ironically, it is we who begin to chase that perfection monster instead of the other way around. The scarier thought becomes, "What if I'm not fast enough to catch it?"

I am afraid that is an irrational fear. No one is fast enough to catch the perfection monster because the perfection monster does not exist. We are chasing a figment of our imagination and just like the rainbow, we never find our imagination's end. No matter how far you run or how fast, you will never out run yourself. So the monster looms larger, getting bigger and bigger as we spend our lives in chase. The result is that we miss all of the magnificent moments along our journey because we are running too fast to see them and are blinded by our pursuit of the imaginary. We run past our lives trying to arrive at Never Never Land.

Do you get how serious that is? We will miss out on living a great life if we remain preoccupied with the fleeting idea of perfection. We will miss out on the only real life we get because we are busy chasing a fantasy. We will miss out on the only real love we get. We will miss out on the only real joy. The only real peace. All because of the monster in our imagination.

It is time to put away childish things. It is time to stop living in fear. No more monsters! (Sorry Lady Gaga.) It is time to experience real-time, right now peace, joy, and love. It begins with slaying that perfectionist monster that keeps you on the run and keeps you from being present in the present. God has provided all of your needs according to His riches in glory by Christ Jesus. Philippians 4:19. But, His provision is in the present. His divine Presence is in the present. You may be surprised to find that your present life is closer to perfect than you ever realized.

56

1) How do you define success?

2) Examine your definition of success. Is there any aspect to your definition that encompasses the idea of perfection?

3) If your definition of success includes perfection, take time to redefine it in a way that does not include the imaginary perfection monster. :)

CHAPTER NINE:

HIS STRENGTH IS MADE PERFECT IN MY WEAKNESS

I am so blessed to have a strong father. He is my hero. He is a faithful man with a sincere heart. He may look a little intimidating on the outside with the permanent furrow in his brow and his white hair. But, he is a teddy bear, no a sweet squishy gummy bear on the inside. You may find this hard to believe, but in elementary school, he used to wake me up every morning and run my bath water. On top of that, he would give me enough time to snooze in the tub and then wake me again when I needed to really hurry up and get dressed. I went through this phase where all I wanted for lunch was popcorn. This was before the days of Pop-Secret Homestyle. He would pop fresh popcorn every morning and even took time out to remove the seeds so I wouldn't hurt myself by chomping down on one. In the winter at bed-time, he would warm my cold sheets and toes with a hand-held blow dryer. My mom, who is awesome too by the way, would often go grocery shopping after an evening church service. My two older brothers and I preferred to stay in the car and have dad tell us a story; he was a fantastic story teller. I had one of those folding door closets. My dad would stand behind the door, holding a stuffed animal at the top and give me an impromptu puppet show! My daddy is awesome!

Let me pause here for a moment to address how unique and precious my experience with my father is. You may be one of the ones who will find that paragraph painful to read because it highlights the absence of a meaningful relationship with your father in your life. I am sorry to be the source of a reminder of your pain. However, I do want to tell you that your Heavenly Father, your creator cares about you beyond what any earthly father can even comprehend. Right now in your life, beyond the realm of what you can see or hear or touch, He is working things out for your good just how my daddy fixed my lunch or warmed my toes. Daddy God cares for you and loves you with a love that surpasses our ability to even know it. Whatever you have gone through, know that Daddy God has a way of taking what the enemy meant to destroy you and working it out for your good. You are who you are today in part because of your past experiences. And, who you are today is exactly who you need to be for God to meet you where you are and bless you. So don't allow these stories to exacerbate your pain. Instead, let them be a reminder to you of how God loves and cares for you. Thanks for the talk. I needed that. :)

This is my all-time favorite story about my dad. Although I was only a two blocks away, my dad typically picked me up from Tierra Del Sol Elementary School. One warm spring day I had worn a little peach and white striped cotton shorts set my mom bought me from Bealls. When the school bell rang, I went and waited in the usual spot, on the sidewalk by the back gate. Hmm. No dad. I figured he was just running a little late and within moments what started as a beautiful blue, partly cloudy sky turned into a gray ominous mess. Rain. Still no dad. I was kind of excited because I figured walking home in the rain would be an adventure. So, off I went. Not so fast! The drops of rain started falling hard, really hard. The wind shifted and began to blow like crazy. Then, the unthinkable. All hail broke loose! The rain turned to hail and started to pelt my skin. I guess trying to walk home wasn't such a great idea after all!

Luckily, there was an office building along the way that had wide pillars. I ducked behind a pillar and tried to use it to block the hail. That was not enough shelter because the wind was whipping around the brick; so I went in. I can only imagine what I looked like. I little soaking wet black girl in the middle of the office, looking like what the cat drug in. I asked if I could use the phone and called home to reach my dad. "Baby, I'm so sorry. Your mom has one car and your brothers took the other car. I did not have a way to pick you up. Stay right there and I will come and get you." Just as fast as it came, the storm left. Before long, my dad came. He had on tall rubber boots so he could walk through the flood and brave the record-setting hail on the ground. My father dressed up for everything! I've seen him work on the roof in his tie and slacks. So for him to put on those rubber boots to come get me was a miracle in and of itself. But, he did just that. When he arrived, he put me on his back and carried me all the way home.

You see I was no match for the storm and hail. I did not have the wherewithal to brave the wind-beaten path back home. I was, in essence, weak. But, my weakness is what paved the way for my father to pick me up, put me on his back, and carry me home. It was my need that allowed him to demonstrate his strength. It was through the storm that I was able to grow my relationship with my dad.

On the day of Pentecost when the Holy Spirit fell on the disciples, they spoke in different languages at the prompting of the Spirit. People were there from various nations and marveled because they heard the disciples who were all from Galilee speaking in the native tongue of their distant homeland. (Acts 2:1-13) Do you know what made this linguistic feat of any interest whatsoever? The limitation of the disciples. Yes, it was their weakness that demonstrated God's strength.

If the disciples had all studied abroad during the previous semester of college and were speaking the language of their ex-patriot experience, no one would be so impressed. So they listened to a month of Rosetta Stone. Big deal! But, that was not the case. The on-lookers recognized that the disciples were not highly educated, well travelled experts in language. Not by a long shot. The only explanation for their speaking in other tongues is supernatural.

It is the lack of the disciples' education that made this moment a miracle to all who beheld. Could it be that we are trying with such fervor to conceal our limitations that we are inadvertently stealing God's opportunity to shine through us? Hands-raised emoji. I am guilty.

I used to think that it was through my "perfection" that God would be glorified. I thought that if I lived an impeccable, mistake-free, exemplary life, people would be able to utilize my life as proof that it is possible to make it unscathed in this world (with God on your side of course). I believed that my perfection would somehow be a reflection of God's glory.

How foolish! Now I realize that it is precisely because of my frailty that the fullness of Christ can be demonstrated through me. To put it plainly, the Light of God shines through cracks in the clay. A solid clay pot with no holes would not only hide the light of a candle, it would extinguish it, robbing it of the very oxygen needed to feed the fire. Likewise, it is the contrast of the darkness of our humanity that puts the spotlight on His divinity. It is the fact that God can use the foolish things to confound the wise that demonstrates His incomprehensible intellectual capacity and irrefutable superiority.

Anyone can raise a king from the succession of kings. Only God can reach down into the gutter of society and pull up a young shepherd boy who had suffered rejection by his own family and make him one of the greatest kings in history! That is how God demonstrated His strength in David's life.

No one bats an eye at a twenty-something, sleeping with her fiancée, getting pregnant and having a baby, but let a 90-year old post-menopausal woman suddenly get pregnant after a lifetime of failed attempts and see how many headlines it inspires. That is how God showed himself strong in the life of Sarah and Abraham.

God saving a super religious Pharisee, "blameless" in keeping the law is cool. But, what about when He saves a "ho-fessional"? (By ho-fessional I mean a member of the oldest profession, a whoremonger, a street-walker, a woman of ill-repute, a prostitute, or maybe a sex-slave.) Never mind the fact that we all have fallen short of the glory of God; and sin is sin. That, right there, would be all up in your Twitter feed! Rahab owned a brothel, was not even Jewish and somehow was used by God to help the Israelites in battle and is one of the few women mentioned in Jesus' lineage. Wow!

I could go on, but you get the point. It is our weakness that demonstrates God's strength. No weakness? No demonstration. Many weaknesses? Many opportunities for God to show Himself to and through you. Does that mean you go sin so God can be revealed? Heck No! Trust me, your natural, every-day setbacks are more than enough to do the trick. But, you must be honest about your weakness for the truth of God's strength to be seen. You must be honest with yourself if you are ever to receive the truth of His love. Ironically, sometimes that love can best be seen during a storm or through His response to our weakness. If you've ever sinned really good (or really badly) and felt His presence comfort you as He whispered, "You are forgiven. I love you still. I haven't changed my mind about your future...," then you know just what I mean.

—— GRACE REFLECTIONS ————————————————————

1) Is there an area in your life where you pretend to be something that you're not? Is there something you use to distract people from your weakness?

2) What do you think would happen if your peers found out the truth about you in that area?

3) Could it be that the weakness you're hiding is an area where God desires to demonstrate His strength?

CHAPTER TEN:

GRACE IS NOT A CREDIT CARD

I don't know about you, but it seems that I am forever getting some kind of credit card offer in the mail. "Take advantage of zero percent APR for the first 12 months when you transfer balances." Zero percent APR sounds free; but, we know better. The moment that you accidentally pay even a few hours past the deadline it shoots up to some ridiculous rate, plus a late fee. Gotcha! You better believe they are banking on you keeping that new balance significantly beyond the zero percent time frame. Besides that, all you're really doing is transferring the debt from one card to another. You are just managing the problem, not eradicating the debt.

Is this how you view grace? As though your right standing with God only lasts for twelve months if you don't mess it up somehow and cut it off even shorter? Best case scenario, you will be here one year from now trying to figure out how to handle your sin debt all over again. Hopefully by then, you would have figured out how to stand on your own two feet and earn your righteousness because the free grace ride is over. It was nice while it lasted. If this is how we view grace, then it is difficult if not impossible for us to actually settle down and live by grace.

Seriously, that is what I thought the message was when I was growing up in the Pentecostal, Apostolic church. Jesus died for your sins, now get it together before you go to hell! If you're really saved, then you don't do this, and you don't do that, and you don't do the other. If you're sinning, you are not saved. You better repent before it is too late. Jesus is coming back like a thief in the night. If you don't get your life right, you're going to get left. On and on they would go preaching with a focus on sin and exclusion from the promises of God. According to that so-called good news, my right standing with God was wholly dependent on my ability to do right. Sure Jesus gives me a head start. But, that's all it is, a head start before all of the onus and responsibility to do and be right falls squarely on my shoulders.

If grace is only a head start on me paying off my own debt, there is no use in even getting started because the sin debt goes beyond what our works could ever pay. Our works are not even the right currency to pay off our sin debt. It is like trying to buy a car with cotton balls. No matter how much you amass, it cannot be exchanged for what you need. If all grace does is give me twelve months without accruing sin interest, then sad to say it is useless. Thankfully, grace is so much more than a transfer of my sin debt from one card which I am responsible for paying to another card that is still in my name.

Grace means that my sin debt is totally annihilated, absolutely forgiven! What's more, not only are my past sins forgiven, my present and future sins are also totally covered by the righteousness of Christ Jesus that is assigned to me by faith. It is justification, not just a vacation. Corny, I know. But, it is true. I will dare quote Wikipedia because they got the definition right:

Justification, in Christian theology, is God's act of removing the guilt and penalty of sin while at the same time declaring a sinner righteous through Christ's atoning sacrifice. In Protestantism, righteousness from God is viewed as being credited to the sinner's account through faith alone, without works. https://en.wikipedia.org/wiki/Justification_(theology)

Now let's look to the Bible:

> *Therefore, having been justified by faith, we have peace with God through our Lord Jesus Christ, through whom also we have access by faith into this grace in which we stand, and rejoice in hope of the glory of God. For when we were still without strength, in due time Christ died for the ungodly. Scarcely for a righteous man will one die; yet perhaps for a good man someone would even dare to die. But God demonstrates His own love toward us, in that while we were still sinners, Christ died for us. Much more then, having now been justified by His blood, we shall be saved from wrath through Him. For if when we were enemies we were reconciled to God through the death of*

His Son, much more, having been reconciled, we shall be saved by His life.
Romans 5:1-2, 6-19 (NKJV)

This scripture says it all doesn't it? First of all, our sin debt has been paid in full e.g. we are justified by faith in our Lord Jesus Christ. The sin debt having been taken care of, we have right standing with God. I love the way this scripture puts it; we have peace with God. There is not an adversarial relationship between you and God. Your sin debt has been eradicated by faith in Jesus Christ. When you make Jesus Lord of your life, something shifts. You no longer stand on the sinking sand of shame, fearfully expecting judgment. Immediately your stance is changed. Through Jesus your feet are placed on the solid rock of grace and you can rejoice in a new hopeful expectation for the glory of God! Hallelujah!

Lest you think this is only a temporary shift, Paul goes on to combat that tendency to believe it is too good to last. Christ died for us while we were sinners. In our worst, most ungodly state, God looked at us and loved us so much that He felt like we were worth dying for! More than a mere sentiment, God demonstrated His love and sent His beloved only son and Christ died for us while we were absolute sinners. Christ's blood is the only acceptable currency to eradicate our sin debt once and for all and it did just that. So we went from being enemies of God to being reconciled, coming back together, having peace with God.

Christ died and used His blood to pay our debt and transform us from sinners to righteous and change our expectation from awaiting judgment to rejoicing in hope of the glory of God. But, now that we have peace with God we are on our own? No way! If His blood bought us peace with God when we were enemies, now that we have a peaceful relationship with God, how much more will we be saved by His life! If Jesus' death was enough to handle our sins and reconcile us, then surely His life is more than enough to keep us.

Paul understood that it would be difficult for people to believe that Christ really is enough. One of the things that is striking is that Paul takes the time to express the degree of Christ's sufficiency.

Level One: We are sinners, far from God and still Christ died for us. Christ's blood has enough power to take us from being so deep in sin debt that we are enemies with God to absolute justification and peace with God.

Level Two: Now we are justified, standing in grace, walking in peace with God, expecting His Glory. Christ's life has much more power to uphold us in this peaceful state, expecting not wrath and judgment, but the glory of God.

If we are rescued through Christ, how much more power does He have to maintain our reconciled life? Much more! The benefits of grace do not dissipate, getting weaker over time. Grace is even more powerful after our reconciliation to God than it was before. Why? Because Jesus is alive! He chose to lay His life down because His blood was the only currency that could pay off our sin debt once and for all. But, Jesus did not stay in the grave. He rose on the third day with all power in His hand. Jesus is much more than enough to save us from ourselves.

1) Is there a part of you that failed to completely buy into the gospel because you felt like you would then be held to a higher level of accountability to which you could not attain?

2) What does the phrase "It's justification, not just a vacation" speak to you?

3) Do you realize that if God's grace is enough to save you, it is more than enough to keep you?

CHAPTER ELEVEN:

FALLING FROM GRACE

For if you are trying to make yourselves right with God by keeping the law, you have been cut off from Christ! You have fallen away from God's grace. Galatians 5:4

Having been blessed with at least the standard amount of balance, I don't typically have an issue with falling down. But, that does not mean I have never fallen. Not once, but twice while in undergrad I was crossing grassy areas in Hampton University's yard. The grass was level at the top. That level grass gave the appearance of the ground beneath likewise being level. Apparently, that was just an optical illusion because unbeknownst to me, looming beneath the tall grass was a pit, a crater that was at least a foot deep in the ground.

I used to host a college radio show that started early in the morning. To accomplish this, every morning that I was on the air I had to go get the keys to the station from the security office, turn on the transmission and start the show by six A.M. In case you were wondering, I am NOT a morning person. I am the type of person who can accidentally stay up passed three in the morning. Needless to say, this early morning aspect to the show was a challenge. If my memory serves me correctly, one time I quickly left the station in the hands of my assistant while I ran back to my dorm to get something I forgot in my early morning haze. Who knows what it was. I was running through the grass to get back to the station and my foot found one of those grassy pits I described. Fortunately, it was so early in the morning that no one was around and I had a soft grassy place to land. I did not just trip. I fell all the way to the ground! The only thing hurt was my ego and maybe my knee.

It's ok; I have two. Flushed, with my heart racing from the unexpected change in elevation, I popped up as fast as I could, looked around and started running again.

Falling never has a good connotation. It is one thing to dive, slide or jump. Those things are intentional. But, falling is an entirely different thing altogether. It is not something done on purpose. It catches you unaware. It can actually cause significant injury to more than just your pride. You could break a bone falling. And, it's embarrassing. I wish I could insert some of the videos I've seen on social media of ridiculously funny falls. There was that big-boned model in Atlanta shaking it with every step until she got to the end of the runway and fell all the way off the stage! Or the graduate in the stacked high heals whose ankles just couldn't take the trip. Falling may provide others with a good laugh. But falling, in and of itself, is never good. In fact, in the elderly population, falling often is the catalyst that leads to a major health crises or even death.

"Fallen from grace" is a phrase we most often hear associated with some kind of really shameful act, the kind that takes a person from famous to infamous, from popular to notorious. Did you hear about that famous television evangelist doing X, Y and Z? What a shame!?! Reverend So-And-So has fallen from grace. Can you believe that this politician was caught sleeping with this person that was not their wife and sexting messages of themselves to his interns? Wow! Senator So-And-So has fallen from grace. The worse the offense, the farther one is thought to have fallen.

As a result of popular usage of the phrase, we think that to fall from grace means to make a huge mistake. Oddly enough, that is not at all the way the Apostle Paul used the phrase when he was writing to the Galatian church. In fact, in a way it has the opposite meaning. Clearly, to fall from grace recognizes that grace is the higher state of being. Grace is superior to whatever one might subsequently fall to. But, what does Paul think is beneath grace? The answer: Trying to make ourselves right with God by keeping the law. Wait. What!?!
According to Paul, you don't fall from grace into sin; you fall from grace into self-effort, trying to make yourself right with God through your own good deeds. SMH. So going from the high place of accepting God's grace as the only way to access the state of being right with God to the lower place where you are trying to earn said right-standing by doing good deeds (keeping the law) is falling. Wow!

You are tripping if you think that you can make yourself right by any good deed. We cannot earn right standing with God. We can only receive it. So get out of your head! It's time for us to stop judging ourselves based on our mistakes and start living by faith in the God who paid for our righteousness through the sacrifice of His only son.

After reading the first draft of this book, someone told me they wished that I would right a book for people that did not commit any great sin, a book for someone who never really messed up in their lives. If you think that you are good enough on your own and nothing you've ever done is that bad, you are missing the point. If you feel that way, you probably have not had the type encounter with a Holy and Perfect God that Isaiah had. When you really encounter the glory of God, His majesty, His eternal greatness, you say like Isaiah 6:5 NLT, "It's all over! I am doomed, for I am a sinful man. I have filthy lips, and I live among a people with filthy lips. Yet I have seen the King, the Lord of Heaven's Armies." The standard is not being a good person in comparison to people with "messed up lives." It is not a class thing or a race thing or a professional thing. It is a comparison to the divine and unsurpassed glory of God. Have you seen those commercials advertising bleach where they are comparing something that is ultra white to something that is supposed to be white? When the supposedly white shirt gets next to the white shirt, you see how not-white it is. For even the best among us, our sins are as scarlet, the deepest red, but through Christ we are washed white as snow!

It does not matter who you are, we all fall short of God's glorious standard. You have not gotten to a place where you no longer need the grace of God. Furthermore, if you are living your life outside of grace, being good enough all on your own, you are in an inferior position. You have fallen and you do not even know it. There are 665 laws in the Old Testament. How can you live by the law when you don't even know the law? Even if you did know it, the law just shows you your sin. That is why we need grace. For no one can ever be made right with God by doing what the law commands. The law simply shows us how sinful we are. Romans 3:20 (NLT)

Grace is not an introductory course in the first year curriculum of an undergraduate degree in righteousness. Grace is the intro course, the mandatory subject of the thesis to earn an Ph.D. and EVERYTHING in between. Grace is the LSAT, the Bar Exam and the challenging three years of law school in between. What I am trying to make clear is that there is no advancement beyond grace. The moment you go from grace to trying to earn your status with God by your own merit, you are falling as hard as Alicia Key's first hit single.

1) Before reading this chapter, what did you think when you heard the phrase "fallen from grace."

2) Be honest, did/do you feel the weight of trying to earn your way into heaven with your own good deeds?

3) How does understanding that dependence on grace is not something to graduate from into a higher state of maturity, but is the highest form of spiritual achievement affect the way you live your life?

CHAPTER TWELVE:

GRACE IN A MERITOCRACY
(TOO GOOD TO BE TRUE)

Webster defines meritocracy as a system in which the talented are chosen and moved ahead on the basis of their achievement. This notion of achievement being the determining factor of one's place in society is often propagated as the "American Way," however accurate or inaccurate as the case may be. The ideology says that you get what you earn. The folks that earn the most do so because they work the hardest or are the smartest and your worth is determined by your quantifiable contribution to the gross national product, America's bottom line.

Never mind the glaring inequity in our history and present. Never mind those that were subsidized by the government to succeed while others were denied access to land ownership and the right to vote. Never mind the bootleggers turned legitimate businessmen that were given an illegal head start. Never mind the raping and pillaging of the Native Americans who were naive enough to lend a helping hand to the pilgrims who would have starved to death without their kindness. The prevailing perception is often that people get what they deserve. And it follows that what you deserve is based on your ability to earn it.

This do-good-to-get-good mentality is imbedded everywhere in our society. It starts before preschool where it is reinforced with a coveted gold stars or happy face stickers earned for good behavior. As I shared earlier, even my second-grade-self was caught up in the perpetual cycle of performance for reward. After all, there was a gum ball to be earned for every week that you didn't get your name on the board for talking out of turn and the like. Then there are your chores that can earn you that allowance, which can buy you those jeans that will make you the person that you have longed to be! I have to be good enough, which equates to: I have to score high enough; I have to be successful enough; I have to make mommy and daddy proud enough.

Do good to get good is the natural order of things. For the most part, I am not knocking it. However, in the face of the meritocratic society in which we live, it seems impossible to really grasp the concept of and therefore live by grace.

Grace is the ultimate rebellion. Grace says, "You don't have to be good enough to get God's blessings." So much more than that, grace is an acknowledgement that you can never be good enough in and of yourself to earn God's blessings. You can never do enough good to earn your way into right standing with God. Never!

Wait a second! What if I go into full Mother Theresa mode and live my whole life doing nothing for myself, but rather caring for the most helpless outcasts in society? That has to be good enough to earn God's favor right? Nope.

What if I fast until I'm skin and bones, meditate every hour of the day that I am awake, and become a spiritual guru, leading thousands of others to draw near to God by suffering? That has to be good enough to earn God's favor. Nuh-uh.

What if I literally sacrifice my life like Will Smith's character in the film 7 Pounds and I find deserving people to donate all of my precious organs to. That must be more than enough to earn God's favor. Nice try. But, not only will that not work, it's also a little weird. No offense.

Why is it that even the most righteous acts and extreme examples of human sacrifice and piety are not enough to earn God's grace? I'm glad you asked. Geez! What took you so long? Let's look to Isaiah 64:6 for the answer; in the New Living Translation it reads:

> We are all infected and impure with sin.
> When we display our righteous deeds,
> they are nothing but filthy rags.
> Like autumn leaves, we wither and fall,
> and our sins sweep us away like the wind.

The thing that we are fighting to overcome within ourselves is not the lack of good deeds. We are fighting a chronic disease, a virus that changes the very nature of our being. You guessed it - SIN. We are all infected and impure because of sin. Untreated, sin disease walls off our heart from God's goodness and the immediate reaction that all of us invariably demonstrate is to try to do something good to counteract the bad. When we become conscious of the sin within ourselves, we try to do something righteous or cover it up. But, that is not how it works.

My nieces and nephew love Band-Aids. I remember being the same way as a child. You have a cut, a scrape, a boo boo of some kind and you need attention! You need some tender loving care to make it feel better. Even when we don't need it, even when it will do nothing to help our hurt, we want a Band-Aid. Just allowing someone to show you enough thoughtfulness and care to pick the perfect sized bandage and place it on your place of pain was major. It made it feel better, whether or not it really had any immediate healing properties.

Our knee-jerk reaction to try to do good deeds to counteract our sin disease is like taking a Band-Aid of self-righteousness and putting it on the cancer of the soul. It may make us feel better for a brief moment. But, it does absolutely nothing to cure the condition. What's worse is that our good deeds in attempt to be righteous aren't like the sterile little flesh-toned bandages we buy from Walgreen's. The scripture says that our righteous deeds are like filthy rags! Let me take a moment to briefly discuss the filthiness of these rags to which our self righteousness is being compared.

WARNING: This is Guaranteed to Gross You Out! Brace yourself. The menstrual cycle of women did not begin with the invention and dissemination of Tampax or Always ultra thin. During the Bible days, women had to use rags to soak up the lining of the uterus that was shed every month they weren't pregnant. After collecting the blood and tissue shed during a woman's period, can you imagine how useless that rag would be for any subsequent use. Let me take these old dried up period rags, wash them and use them for. . . NO!!! Those rags are done! They are the definition of FILTHY.

So when we try to do good in hopes of offsetting the balance of our sin disease, it is taking something as vile and disgusting as the disease itself, placing it on top of our impurity like a filthy Band-Aid on cancer and expecting it to bring healing. It does not even make sense. Now excuse me while I gargle from having thrown up just a little in my mouth. Blah!

There is something else that I find fascinating about this verse. Like autumn leaves, we whither and fall, and our sins sweep us away like the wind. I've never seen this connection before. The imagery of shriveling leaves makes me think of Adam and Eve in the Garden of Eden. Their solution to their sin and the resulting discovery of their nakedness was to sow fig leaves together to cover themselves. These fig leaves were beginning to wither before they could even sow together their fruit of the loom.

The leaves represent the solution of self righteousness and they are no match for the power of sin. The leaves begin dying as soon as you separate them from the vine. In this metaphor, sin is the wind that will blow away these shrunken, dying, dry attempts of self-righteousness before you even know it! You will think you're covered and the shriveled leaves will not only be exposing your nakedness, they will shine a spotlight on the very areas that you do not want anyone to see.

That is why our good deeds cannot earn us right standing with God. Accepting the gift of grace is an acknowledgement that there is nothing that we can do to fix our sin disease. Our best efforts are grossly inadequate, therefore we need to be rescued because we cannot save ourselves. There are no exceptions to this rule. Under no circumstances can we save ourselves. Enter Grace stage left. While every other part of our society in every other aspect of our lives is telling us that we have to earn it to get it, grace is flipping that mentality on its head. Grace says, "You cannot do this on your own; therefore, I am coming to the rescue."

What must we do to access the benefits of this free gift? Just receive it as such. Don't pretend to have earned it. Don't act like you worked for it. Whatever you do, don't walk around as though you deserve it. Recognize it for what it is, an unmerited gift, given by the Most-High God in order for Him to reconcile your relationship with Himself. You simply cannot earn it. Stop trying. God is calling you to get off the hamster wheel of good-works-to-get-right-with-God and simply receive the gift of God that is Grace.

I am not advocating for all people everywhere to cease performance of all good works. What I am saying is that good works are not an effective treatment for sin

FIFTY SHADES OF GRACE

disease and therefore do not earn your salvation. The only cure to sin cancer is the divine prescription of Grace. For the wages of sin is death, but the free gift of God is eternal life through Christ Jesus our Lord. Romans 6:23 (NLT). When you punch the time-clock of sin, you're earning something. It doesn't matter how long your lunch break may be, sin comes with wages. It does not matter the level of the sin, you earn a one-size fits all wage, death. Death/separation from life is the direct repercussion of sin.

Conversely, you cannot earn eternal life through Jesus Christ. It is a free gift. Once you have received that free gift, you do good deeds because you are righteous, not to attain righteousness. You can exercise the effort to reach your goals out of a place of success, not to obtain success. You don't have to work for these things. You can instead work from a foundation of grace and know from the beginning that you have already won!

1) Is there a part of you that is trying to do good to counteract the bad?

2) What kinds of things have you done in attempt to make up for your sin?

3) Have you ever really received God's grace and accepted it as enough for YOU? If not, what is stopping you?

CHAPTER THIRTEEN:

THE WORK GOD WANTS FROM YOU

I lived in Los Angeles, California for three years during my leap-of-faith/starving artist days. It is a long story that is better suited for another time and place. I had a love hate relationship with LA. I love the diversity and the beauty that is everywhere. Even the sidewalks downtown sparkle with possibility. There is so much amazing talent there; you cannot throw a rock without hitting a world class musician or writer or actor or... And the food! All kinds of amazing restaurants that taste like home if you were from Thailand or Jamaica or... It really is amazing! The hate was due in part to there being a concentration of con artists and people that want to take advantage of you. It's like you always have to be on guard, lest you become the next victim of fraud. And the drivers! This next story combines two of the things I hate about LA.

To cut to the chase, I had a dent in my car from a driver that was high out of his mind on weed. I chose not to call the cops because he gave this long sob story about how his mom and brother died and he was on probation, yada, yada. He even lifted up his shirt and showed me a tattoo that covered his entire back featuring his mother holding he and his brother as little boys on her lap. Moving right? Can you believe he hired a lawyer and tried to sue me after my kindness prevented me from getting his behind thrown in jail no less! Fortunately, at the time of the accident, I recorded a video on my phone and made him admit to the accident being his fault. You could also see that he was high in the video, thick tongued, slightly incoherent. It was a masterpiece! LOL That's what Spike Lee would've done right? I'm not one hundred percent certain, in part because I had a number of fender benders in the city of angels, but I believe it was this same dent that garnered the attention of a fast talking guy outside in the Ralph's parking lot.

He was with a couple other guys and explained in a thick accent that he would remove the dent from my door and make it as good as new for just $200. He said that he was borrowing a piece of equipment from his boss for the day and that's why he was willing to do the work so inexpensively. He had to turn the equipment back in tomorrow so I didn't have much time to make the decision. I was very hesitant, but he assured me that if he didn't make it look exactly like the other side I would not owe him a dime.

Since I didn't have to pay unless I was totally satisfied, what did I have to lose? I know you can predict what happened. If it is possible to make the already dented door look worse, that is exactly what he did. Then when I reminded him that he said I didn't have to pay unless he made the door look exactly like the one on the other side, he protested vociferously and made it seem as though I was being unfair. "I wish I had a recording of what I said before," he contended, outraged and demonstrative. I felt very threatened by him and his friends. Under duress, I paid him even though my door looked like crap. It was basically robbery. SMH.

Maybe by now you are remembering the old adage your mother used to say, "If it seems too good to be true, it probably is." That is true for most things in life, but not for the gospel. I would contend that if it does not seem too good to be true, it probably is not the gospel. However, while we can never earn the free gift that is eternal life, that doesn't mean there is no work for us to do whatsoever. There is work to be done. It just doesn't come in the form that you would expect.

One day, some of the people in the crowd that followed Jesus who were enamored by His miraculous works, namely the multiplication of the fish and loaves, told Jesus they too wanted to do God's works. The question was what they had to do to be able to do the works of God. Jesus' response to them speaks volumes and is just as if not more relevant to us today. It is found in John 6:28-29 New King James Version:

> Then they said to Him, "What shall we do, that we may work the works of God?" Jesus answered and said to them, "This is the work of God, that you believe in Him whom He sent."

In the New Living Translation, the 29th verse says this, Jesus told them, "This is the only work God wants from you: Believe in the one he has sent." So I don't have to climb Mount Kilimanjaro? I don't have to memorize the Pentateuch (aka the first five books of the Bible)? I don't have to give my body to be burned? The only "work" God wants from me is to "believe in the one he has sent." That's it!?! All I have to do is believe? That is the fullness of my responsibility to act in response to the reality of Jesus. Just believe? No way!

I like the way the New King James Version really captures human nature regarding the desire and belief that we have to earn the privilege to do God's will. In essence, these unnamed members of the crowd were saying, "What do we have to do to in order to earn the opportunity to…" This question assumes that there is a barrier of entry. In their mind, there was no way they could go from zero to 100. Coming from their orthodox background, they probably assumed there was some type of purification ritual, some sacrifice or series of sacrifices to be made. Maybe they had to desert their current life and serve several years in the temple first.

In their mind, whatever sacrifice was demanded came as a prerequisite, that was just to pave the way to earn the ability to work the works of God. So they thought they had to work in order to work the works. Whew! I am exhausted just saying that. What are you doing with your life? Working hard so that one day I can work the works. Wait. What!?!

I recently went to my youngest niece's kindergarten graduation. Each cute, mini human had to come to the microphone and say what they liked best about their kindergarten experience. Out of all of the baby graduates, little London was the very first to the mic, "What I liked most was (drum roll please this is my niece's big moment) the work." Blink. Blink. Oh no! She's already a workaholic at five years old! Maybe she said that because she really enjoyed her assignments. Or, maybe it is that doing the work made her feel like her big sisters Kameron and Alexx who she admires and had seen toil over homework into the evening. Doing work can make you feel like you are doing something important, something necessary. Doing work can make you feel like a grown up, earning your place in the world.

But, Jesus does not give them some long list of things they had to work to do in order to gain entry into working these next level works. Instead, He took the S off of works and made it singular. There is only one work that God wants from you. One work. What is it? Simply believe in the one [God] sent. Jesus, of course, was speaking of himself. The only work that God wants from us, the only work that pleases Him is to believe in Jesus! God doesn't want all of these religious practices and acts of self-righteousness; God wants you to believe in Jesus.

Hebrews 11:6 in the New King James Version tells us just how important belief is: "But without faith it is impossible to please Him, for he who comes to God must believe that He is, and that He is a rewarder of those who diligently seek Him." So our only job is to respond to Jesus with faith. The only work I am responsible for is to believe that: (1) God exists; and (2) That He is a rewarder of those who diligently seek Him. If you believe that, then it will result in you coming to God. If you believe that God is real and is longing to bless those in an authentic relationship with Him, you would be motivated to go after God with your entire being.

Finding Jesus is the ultimate reward. Having a genuine, committed relationship with the Creator, the lover of your soul is the best thing ever. However, there are so many more blessings than you can imagine awaiting your pursuit of a relationship with God through Jesus Christ. All you really have to do to to attain this reward is to believe in Him, the one who God sent. The rest will come naturally. Just believe.

—— GRACE REFLECTIONS ————————————————

1) Do you believe in Jesus?

2) If so, do you recognize that your belief in him is enough to grant you access to living a life that is empowered by Christ?

3) What have you been trying to add to your faith in God in order to earn God's favor?

CHAPTER FOURTEEN:

FAITH CYCLE

Let's go back in time to the patronistic system in Rome. If you recall, the term grace described a socio-economic system in which a patron would grant a favor to a client who reciprocated with gratitude. Faith is the currency that runs this exchange of grace. Faith was a common word to the people who lived and worked within this patronistic world. Like grace, faith is multifaceted, but was not necessarily a religious word. A type of faith had to be demonstrated by the patron and the client alike in order for the relationship to work.

The very foundation of the patronage system is the faithfulness of the patron. The patron establishes his worth by having demonstrated his power and influence together with fidelity to his word. The patron must actually have the requisite power to carry out the favor and be faithful to do what was promised. Not only is he capable, powerful and influential enough to accomplish the task at hand, if he said he would do it, you can count it as done. It is interesting to note that the patron's faithfulness is once more a by-product of his benevolent character and exists independent of the existence of any particular client. The value of the patron is in his faithfulness.

The client, in turn had to demonstrate faith in two ways, both inextricably tied to the patron. First, the client had to "keep faith" meaning they had to be loyal to the patron and loyal to their unspoken inner oath of displaying gratitude outwardly towards the patron. Second, the client must have faith that the patron is able to fulfill the promise, is willing to show their favor and will in fact perform what they said they would do. You cannot keep faith if you don't first have faith. How can one hold their course, remain faithful, and not jump ship if they don't believe that the route they are on is going to take them where they want to go? In order to be unwavering in one's allegiance to the patron and to intentionally place that devotion on display for all to see, one must believe that it is worth it. The client had to believe the patron had what it takes and cared about them enough to indeed make it happen for them.

What's more, without faith in the patron, the client would never even come to him asking for help. Why would I go to my five-year-old niece to help me with my taxes? She may be willing, but she is not able. Conversely, why would I approach my most outspoken hater and earnestly ask for words of affirmation? They may be able, but they aren't willing. So the client even demonstrates faith in the patron by coming to them in seeking aid in the time of need.

So faith is the token that sets the merry-go-round of grace in motion. Simultaneously, faith has a conversion cycle of its own. The patron may be powerful and influential standing alone. The patron may have a general sense of good will, a loving kindness towards others simply as a self-contained aspect of his character, independent of any specific person towards whom to show it. The patron may be faithful to perform his word. However, it is the faith of the potential client that acts as the deposit, pointing and releasing the patron's faithfulness towards them. In turn, being a recipient of the patron's faithfulness legitimizes and increases the client's faith aka trust in the patron's faithfulness. And it is the increase of that trust that empowers the client to keep faith and stay loyal and grateful, even while waiting on the promise to materialize.

It is grace for grace. It is faith for faith. The system is both elegant and complex. It is founded on the strength and integrity of the patron and his willingness to show favor freely. But, that strength and integrity is activated by a request from a client. Just as the request activates the patron's readiness to give a free gift, receiving the free gift triggers a free-will response of gratitude in the client.

No one is obligated to do anything. Neither the giving nor the receiving is forced. Nothing is required by law: not the gift or the gratitude. It is all beautifully passed back and forth in an elegant, free-flowing dance of grace and faith. It is poetry in motion, perfect in its symmetry.

Our Response

Grace is the love that paved the way for unmerited favor freely given to us by God through Jesus Christ. Grace is the giving. Grace is the gift. But, the Gospel of Grace speaks to more than just this unidirectional sovereign act. It is also about the recipient of divine grace responding with grace and entering into a grace relationship with Grace Himself. It's like the model we learned from the water cycle as kids. The water on the surface of the earth evaporates only to ultimately return to the earth as rain or some other form of precipitation. That is water for water. Here, we are talking grace for grace. God showers down His grace on us. In the warmth of His love, grace goes back to Him as vapors of our gratitude and devotion only for more grace to fall and the cycle continues.

Back to The Godfather, remember that he was insulted when all Bonasera wanted was his favor and not his friendship? You cannot expect to obtain grace from the patron and not have a relationship with him. Just like the Godfather, it pleases God the Father for us to walk in relationship with him. In John 15:15 (NLT) Jesus says, I no longer call you slaves, because a master doesn't confide in his slaves. Now you are my friends, since I have told you everything the Father told me. Just like the earthly patron would graciously call his client friend, through Jesus we are the friends of God! Ultimately, God wants an authentic grace relationship with each one of us. It is His desire that we live a happy and fulfilled life through grace.

God the Father has already done His part in giving the ultimate gift of grace in the person of Jesus Christ, grace personified. The only variable in the equation is our response. God has freely given us grace. We can respond by graciously accepting the gift of His friendship and living a life that demonstrates our gratitude. OR, we can reject grace and try to earn everything in this life on our own, essentially becoming disgrace personified.

When we hear about a person living a life of disgrace, maybe we picture a drug dealer, an addict, an atheist or a devil worshipper. However, anyone who does not respond properly to the grace of God is living a life of disgrace, that not only includes people who totally reject God and His grace through Jesus Christ. It also includes people who self-identify as Christians and still try to earn their right standing with God by keeping the law. It also includes people who self-identify as Christians and yet reject the love of God, the gifts of protection, provision, purpose, identity, comfort, peace, joy and/or security because they do not believe t they deserve it. Living beneath your privilege as a friend of God is a disgrace.

A proper response to God's amazing grace is living a gratified life that is a reflection of that grace. If God gave us peace through grace, then living a life filled with anxiety is a rejection of His perfect gift. If God gave us joy through grace, then to live depressed and forlorn is a disgrace. If God provided our needs through grace, then living in lack is a disgrace. I am not claiming that because of grace our life will be problem free. That would be a lie. What I am saying is that we have a duty to exercise our faith in the grace of God so that we can walk in the manifestation of every benefit that comes with being a friend of God.

Gratitude

Gratitude is the natural response to being a recipient of the gift of grace from God the patron. Again, this is not so much an obligation, not something that you have to do. Gratitude is the reciprocation of grace. Gratitude is the call of grace echoing from your heart, reflecting the gift of grace that was freely given to you. Gratitude is a grace reflex. You know how it is when the doctor hits that perfect spot on your knee. You cannot help but kick your foot out. Likewise, gratitude is something that should come as a direct result of grace hitting that spot of need in our lives.

As mentioned above, there are three facets to the gratitude demonstrated by a friend of the patron. First, they were expected to use whatever means they had to make the patron famous by publicly honoring the patron, testifying to the gift and the benevolent character of the giver. In our relationship with God, this translates to praise and thanksgiving. You cannot silently or privately publicly honor or testify to the gift and the character of God. You have to open up your mouth and speak it. There is no other way.

Therefore, by Him let us continually offer the sacrifice of praise to God, that is, the fruit of our lips, giving thanks to His name. Hebrews 13:15 (NKJV) If you have received the grace of God, if you understand who Jesus Christ is, if you recognize that you are a recipient of the love of God, you cannot help but be grateful. That gratitude should naturally be given a voice. That voice should express praise and thanksgiving to God the Father, honoring him for the ultimate gift and for who He is.

Just like our fingerprints, our voice is totally unique and can be used to identify us from the other seven billion people on earth. It means something when you employ your one-of-a-kind voice in offering praise to God. Your voice matters. If you are not using your voice to express praise and thanksgiving to God, it is because you have not yet gained an understanding of Jesus Christ or recognized the life-changing meaning of grace. Someone reading this is afraid that in order to praise God you will have to look and sound like some crazy or weird person that you do not want to be like. Not so! You can open up your mouth and express praise in your own authentic uniqueness. God did not give us individual voices so that we could force our praise into a monotone box. Praise him in your own way. But, if gratitude is in your heart, you will open up your mouth and give him praise.

Likewise, you will give him credit for your success when you recognize that He is the source of every good and perfect gift in your life. When our accomplishments garner recognition, we are to tell them about how God made a way. As it states in Matthew 5:16, Let your good deeds shine out for all to see, so that everyone will praise your heavenly Father. How can our good deeds be the impetus for people to praise God if we absorb all the admiration for ourselves? When people recognize goodness in us, that is our opportunity to point to our heavenly Father as the source so they will see God in our goodness and praise him!

The second facet of gratitude to the patron is loyalty in support of and affiliation with the patron, even when said affiliation is inconvenient. That means that the echo of grace in our hearts will cause us to live a life of worship, that is to devote our entire lives to God the Father. Paul, the writer of Romans 12:1 expresses this principle this way in the New Living Translation:

> And so, dear brothers and sisters, I plead with you to give your bodies to God because of all he has done for you. Let them be a living and holy sacrifice— the kind he will find acceptable. This is truly the way to worship him.

Praise is something that you do with your mouth, with your hands, with your physical body. Worship is something you do with your entire being; it is living a life of devotion. To give yourself entirely to God, to let it be known that you are a friend of God, to be an ambassador for God, this is loyalty; this is worship.

The third facet of gratitude is service. A client of the patron was to look for any opportunity to give back to the patron by performing a service or giving a gift. How much more should we look for opportunities to give and serve the Ultimate

Patron, God the father! All too often, those of us who call ourselves Christians are not looking for an opportunity to serve and give, instead we are looking for an opportunity to be served and to receive. This insatiable, narcissistic, self-centered desire to receive is disgraceful; it interrupts the flow of grace in our lives. If we are grateful for what has been given, we don't just keep asking for more as though the gift was wholly inadequate to meet our needs. **A real relationship requires reciprocity.**

Giving is an expression of gratitude. Service is an expression of gratitude. We should not just stand around idly by waiting for a need so big that we cannot ignore it and a pitch so irresistible that it finally convinces us to get off of our behind and do a tiny little something to give from what we have already been given. No! If you have ever received God's love and grace, then giving and serving is a natural byproduct of that experience.

In Matthew 6 in the New Living Translation, Jesus is quoted to have said it this way: "Don't store up treasures here on earth, where moths eat them and rust destroys them, and where thieves break in and steal. Store your treasures in heaven, where moths and rust cannot destroy, and thieves do not break in and steal. Wherever your treasure is, there the desires of your heart will also be." Take a moment and think about it. What you spend your money on and give your life to serving is undeniably where your heart is.

If you are not a giver and a server, what I am about to say may make you change your mind about this book that you have enjoyed so thoroughly up until this point. However, I would like to encourage you to keep reading because we are going to talk about faith next and I promise it will bless you! This is going to bless you too. Brace yourself. Are you ready? Ok. Here it goes: Do not say you have a heart for God if you do not give the things that you value to him because the place that you store your treasure is the exact place which has your heart. Don't get mad at me. Jesus is the one who said it. The New King James Version puts Jesus' words this way, "For where your treasure is, there your heart will be also." Not only should giving and serving our heavenly Father be a natural part of our grace response of gratitude, it is a litmus test for the condition of our heart.

Gratitude is the response of our heart to any gift that we deem precious. That gratitude should manifest as praise, a life of devotion (worship), giving and service to God. But, you cannot effectively do any of these things without faith. Let's talk about it.

Faith

The entire grace exchange is set in motion through faith. God our Father is faithful to do what He promised and we must believe that in order to even begin to enter into a grace relationship with him. It is His word that spoke heaven and earth into being. It is His word that spoke light into existence. It is God's word that created our universe from nothing. And, it is His word that was made flesh and became grace personified in the person of Jesus Christ. God has very few limitations, but there is one, He cannot lie. Numbers 23:19 in the New Living Translation says, God is not a man, so he does not lie. He is not human, so he does not change his mind. Has he ever spoken and failed to act? Has he ever promised and not carried it through?

I believe that the reason God does not lie is because He cannot lie. As the speaking Creator, power over every element of the universe is in His voice. Therefore, even if He were to say something that is not yet true, the atoms, molecules, matter and anti-matter would immediately begin lining up to bring His word to pass, instantaneously making it the truth! God could not lie even if He wanted to. When God speaks, He only speaks truth. Say it with me, "God is faithful!" God has absolute fidelity to His word because every object in the universe is at His command. Because God is faithful, He is worthy of our faith in him.

As stated above, the client had to both: (1) "Keep faith" meaning be loyal to the patron and display gratitude outwardly towards the patron; and (2) Have faith that the patron is able to fulfill the promise, is willing to show their favor and will in fact perform what they said they would do. The concept of keeping faith overlaps with that of gratitude, which we already covered. However, the concept of having faith is something we have not yet discussed that directly translates into our faith in God, the ultimate patron.

I don't know about you, but I find shows like Forensic Files captivating, one of my parents' favorites is Dateline. Both shows walk you through the process whereby detectives and scientists are able to solve murders when there is no eye witness and the killer seemed to have left behind little to no evidence.

Through forensic science, things such as DNA evidence and microscopic fibers from a carpet are able to be extracted and used to gather information about the criminal and circumstances of the crime. It's amazing how just a little bit of skin under the fingernails or residue from a shoe imprint could be enough to track down the unknown suspect. What's more, these things are usually imperceptible to our senses, invisible to the human eye. Yet, somehow this is the very evidence used to get the type of information that can uncover the identity of the unseen.

In the New King James Version Hebrews 11:1 says, "Now faith is the substance of things hoped for, the evidence of things not seen." Faith is like spiritual forensic science. Faith is the invisible evidence left by God of His promise until you become an eye witness. You may not see the thing you are hoping for now. But, there is something beyond our five senses that assures us of the reality of our hope in God. That is faith. If you stay in faith long enough, you will see the thing that was once invisible become reality. You will go from spiritual forensics to becoming an eye witness of the manifestation of your faith.

Faith is the founding principle of the universe. By faith we understand that the worlds were framed by the word of God, so that the things which are seen were not made of things which are visible. Hebrews 11:3 (NKJV). That means before there was a world, there was faith. Before the world came to existence, there was a God who was faithful.

Although many point to Hebrews 11:1 as the definitive Bible verse on faith, I find that Hebrews 11:6 provides a more readily understandable explanation of faith: But without faith it is impossible to please Him, for he who comes to God must believe that he is, and that he is a rewarder of those who diligently seek Him. Do you see it? It's as though the writer of Hebrews was providing a two-part definition of faith. Faith is believing that: (1) God is; and (2) That He is a rewarder of them that diligently seek Him.

At The University of Texas School of Law, I learned in my first-year criminal law class that there are certain crimes that require proof of a particular mental state in order to establish the guilt of the actor. Title 5 of the Texas Penal Code Section, 19.02 defines murder; paragraph (2)(b) states in part:

(b) A person commits an offense if he:

(1) intentionally or knowingly causes the death of an individual;

If a prosecutor wants a jury to find someone guilty of murder under this particular provision, they must prove that the accused intentionally or knowingly caused the death of an individual. That specific intent or knowledge is known as the culpable mental state. While there are other ways to commit murder, without the intent or knowledge, the same actions that lead to the death of an individual could not be murder under this provision without that state of mind. Why not? Because the mental state matters.

Faith is the mental state required to please God. You can go through the motions and act like a saint, but without faith as the motivating factor, it does not work. But, what is faith in this context? First of all, faith is a verb, that is believing or to believe. Merriam-Webster defines believe as to accept or regard (something) as true. What does faith in God accept or regard as true? That God is and that God is a rewarder of them that diligently seek him.

It is the acceptance of the truth of God's existence coupled with the acceptance of the truth of His intention and ability to reward those who diligently seek him that is the mental state that motivates our response to God's invitation to enter into a relationship with him. Because we believe that God exists, desires to and will bless those who come to him, we, in turn take a risk and come to him. If we hold as true the fact that God exists and rewards those in a relationship with him, then we also believe that He is able to do what He said He would do, that He will ultimately perform what He promised. In turn, based on holding those things to be true about God, we are motivated to enter into a relationship with him. We believe and we act on that belief. That, my friend, is faith.

Faith is an internal action that causes an internal and external reaction. Faith is the internal act of believing that is demonstrated in the internal and external acts of coming to God. Faith is more than just a catalyst to accepting the invitation to enter a relationship with God; that is the tip of the iceberg. After crying all night long, faith will cause you to wipe the tears from your eyes, put on your make-up, walk out the door and smile because you know that while weeping may endure for a night, joy comes in the morning. Faith will cause you to sacrifice and work hard in order to study in school because you know that God has something good for you on the other side of that degree. Faith will ignite the courage to start your business or pursue your dream although it seems so far away. You are empowered to stay on your grind, to not give up because you know that you know that God is

and He has your reward. That is faith!

I heard Pastor Bill Winston say it this way, "Faith is confidence in God." How succinct! What a power-packed definition in a nutshell. God is faithful and is worthy of our confidence in him!

CHAPTER FIFTEEN:

FIRST THINGS FIRST

Maybe you're still not convinced that grace is not some new fandangle concoction thought up by progressive Christians in order to justify their failure. Let me assure you that from Genesis on God was setting the stage for Jesus, grace personified. This is not some new concept. It is what God had in mind from the very beginning. This next section will walk you through the Bible from Adam to Jesus in a very broad stroke so you can see the thread of grace that holds our Bible together.

Adam & Eve

It all started with Adam and Eve. Oops, I just lost the skeptics. Stick with me while I lay this foundation. This is my version of the Cliffs Notes. Adam and Eve were created by God to be like Him, to enjoy an intimate friendship with Him and were placed in a paradise designed with them in mind. No, I don't think there were dinosaurs in the Garden of Eden; the timing is all wrong. Neither do I believe the earth just randomly is the perfect distance from the sun to sustain life. Science, when rightly interpreted can only verify the truth and help us understand the processes God's spoken word set in motion, but that is another book. The only thing that Adam and Eve had to do was live their life to the fullest, enjoy an uncomplicated relationship with the creator and care for the garden. Oh, and not eat from the tree of the knowledge of good and evil or else they would die. It was *all good*, literally.

But, apparently following that one guideline is more difficult than it sounds because before we know it, both Adam and Eve indulge in the forbidden fruit and paradise, a utopia of uncomplicated and uninhibited communion with the God whose image they were designed to reflect, is lost. With one act of disobedience, sin enters the world. Immediately, they begin to see themselves as flawed and try to come up with their own solutions to cover their newly-discovered inadequacy. While fig leaves can grow to be rather large, the fruit of the loom they sowed together was insufficient to really cover their shame. We know this because when God returned to the Garden to spend some time with the crown jewel of His creation, rather than their usual response of running to meet Him and basking in His presence, they hid. That is what sin does. It separates us from God because it changes our nature. How we see ourselves and how we perceive our maker is altered by our ambitious acts of independence from Him. Eve was already made in God's image, yet she broke the rules in order to "be like God, knowing good and evil." What started off as *all good* became good and evil.

Let's not rush past this. The Genius that created the universe surely knew of their disobedience. In a moment, He could have destroyed everything, the sun, the moon, planet earth, Adam and Eve. But, instead He comes down to meet them on their level. He desires a real relationship and that is something that cannot be coerced or demanded. God came to man in pursuit of his heart and called to them, asking "Where are you?" He did not ask the question because His divine GPS could not find their location. He asked in order to engage with mankind, inviting him to discover himself and confess his sin. Adam answers that he is hiding because he is afraid due to his nakedness. Wait. I thought he covered his nakedness with fig leaves? Nope, not good enough. Man-made adaptations, being a good person, doing good deeds, being spiritual, pretending that you don't hear God calling you, etc. are all incapable of solving the problem of sin. As a result, we shrink back from the light lest it further illuminate our flaws. That shrinkage must have gotten all the way into Adam and Eve's DNA because now every member of the human family is born with it. It is an inner chasm, separating us from that holistic relationship with God that we were originally created for.

Back to Adam and Eve naked, hiding in the bushes. That had to be uncomfortable. How does God respond to their sin? First, He revokes their all-access pass to the Eden Paradise Resort and points out the consequences of their choice. Then, He sacrifices an innocent animal to make leather outfits for Adam and Eve. But, it was not about fashion. It was about the exchange of death and blood for the sin of humanity. God did what was necessary to cover them. It is our first glimpse of the principle articulated in Romans 6:23, sin always comes with a paycheck that none of us want to cash - death. The wages of sin is death. Sometimes death comes quickly, but it is often the slow death and deterioration of us piece by piece, the dead and dying parts weighing us down while we struggle to survive. Think *The Walking Dead* or whatever your favorite zombie reference might be. **Sin causes us to walk around trying to hold our dying selves together while disconnected from the source of life itself.** So this unsuspecting animal, chewing cud stress-free in this vegan paradise is suddenly slain to cover Adam and Eve's sin. It was only the first animal to give his life in what would become the blood bath of human existence.

Abraham

Fast forward about 20 extraordinarily long Bible generations to Abram. The Most-High God is still on His epic quest to not only know His creation, but to be known by them. God is still desperately longing for an intimate relationship with the ones He made in His image, despite their gross misuse/abuse of themselves against His will. In attempt to introduce himself and expose His character to a man and his wife and ultimately to all of humanity, God interrupts the life of an aged man by the name of Abram. Abram was rich. But, we all know that there are things that money cannot buy. For Abram, that elusive thing that he could not acquire no matter how much wealth he amassed was a baby of his own, an heir who would carry on his name and enjoy all that Abram had worked so hard for. It was too late now, because Sarai, his wife although extraordinarily beautiful was far beyond child baring years. He appreciated the financial freedom and all that came with it, but would have traded it in a heartbeat for a son.

God enters stage left and makes a 75-year-old Abram a promise,
> *1 Leave your native country, your relatives, and your father's family, and go to the land that I will show you." 2 I will make you into a great nation. I will bless you and make you famous, and you will be a blessing to others. 3 I will bless those who bless you and curse those who treat you with contempt. All the families on earth will be blessed through you.* Genesis 12:1-3 NLT.

Later God once again came down to earth, made His presence known and met Abram in a culturally relevant way. God assured Abram that His promises were reliable by making a covenant (ancient oath of agreement) with him. God instructed Abram to take five animals and prepare them as the custom required. Not so incidentally, five is the number that represents grace. Once more, blood is shed and God meets a man right where he is.

25 years later, after much heartache and many missteps on Abram, aka Abraham's part, Sarai, now Sarah gives birth to a healthy baby boy, Isaac at 90 years old. Sarah was 90, not the baby. This is the Bible, not Benjamin Button. Can you imagine the joy? The relief Abraham must have felt knowing that he was not crazy, God really did speak to him. God really did make him a promise. God really did what He said He would do! Conversely, can you relate to the dismay Abraham felt when the very same voice that promised him a son spoke again saying, *Take your son, your only son—yes, Isaac, whom you love so much—and go to the land of Moriah. Go and sacrifice him as a burnt offering on one of the mountains, which I will show you.* Genesis 22:2.

Wait a minute. Stop! That makes no sense. Why would God promise Abraham a son just to have him slit his throat on the side of a mountain? That is beyond cruel. That is sadistic! But, how could he not be willing to offer up the precious gift back to the giver? How could he withhold the very thing which was given so freely to him? Abraham, in a heroic act of faith and trust, saddled a donkey and headed towards the mountain. They traveled for three days when Abraham saw the ordained place. Isaac could not help but notice the lack of a sacrificial animal: he was carrying the wood on his back, his dad had the knife, and the fire, but there was nothing to burn. Little did he know the heart of his father was burning within him. To cut to the chase, they arrived, set up the altar and Abraham placed Isaac where the sacrifice should go. Abraham took the knife and raised it up. But, just then, when Abraham grabbed the knife to shed his son's blood on the altar, God stopped him from laying a hand on the boy. *Do not hurt him in any way, for now I know that you truly fear God. You have not withheld from me even your son, your only son.* Genesis 22:12. Thank God!

Just then Abraham saw a ram caught by his horns in a thicket. That ram became the sacrifice that he offered to the Lord. So God had a different plan the entire time! He never intended for Abraham to offer Isaac, He only wanted to know that

His relationship with Abraham was real, that he did not prize the gifts over the giver. Hallelujah. But, this really was a foreshadowing of the truth that was to be made manifest in Jesus. Think about it. You have an only beloved son carrying wood on his back to the hill where his father would forsake him. That sounds a lot like what happened to Jesus. One interpretation for what Abraham called the place is "The Lord Will Provide." He didn't call it the Lord Already Provided. Wouldn't that make more sense in this context? Perhaps the reason is because he was not naming the place for what had already occurred. He was naming it for what would one day occur when Jesus stepped on the scene. Maybe he was saying, "The next time you see something that looks like this, that is God making a way!" Forgive me; I'm getting ahead of myself.

There is so much juicy goodness that I am leaving out of this story for brevity's sake. But, what I want you to see is God taking the initiative to meet man right where he is, providing what man could never attain on his own. You should also take not of the crimson thread that is slowly pulling fallen man towards a perfect God one stitch at a time.

The Death Penalty
Fast-forward even further and you find that God fulfilled His promise; Abraham's descendants became a nation in their own right. First, God made Adam and Eve and came down to them, even after the fall, on a level that they could relate to, reconciling their relationship through the blood of an innocent animal. Then, God chose Abraham and paved the way for him to enter into a covenant relationship with Himself through blood. Next, God, likewise chose the nation that was born of Abraham's seed and under the leadership of Moses instituted The Law.

The Law included the Ten Commandments, which served to show the people their sins and their interrelated need for propitiation. There were 613 laws, requirements to enter into and remain in good standing with God. How could they even remember 613 laws much less comply with them!? 100 of these laws related to the practice of animal sacrifice as a means to produce a continuous flow of blood to establish their status as a nation set apart for God and to make up for their sin.

For you are a holy people, who belong to the Lord your God. Of all the people on earth, the Lord your God has chosen you to be his own special treasure. Deuteronomy 7:6.

Allow me to warn you: this is a bit heavy. The cycle of death went on and on and on. It was a cycle of trying to be good enough, trying to please God enough, trying to make God happy enough. But, it was never enough. The sacrifice was only as good as the time frame it was intended to cover. Therefore, day after day, week after week, month after month, season after season, year after year these same sacrifices had to be brought to the altar as if there were no prior blood shed. That was the problem. No matter how many times you go through the ritual, you have to go through it all over again. That is because the sacrifice of animals was never meant to have a lasting effect on the offeror.

Such ritualistic sacrifices were really just a temporary fix. The sacrifices were merely a foreshadowing of a permanent, perfect solution to sin. Let's take a look at what it took to satisfy the endless need for ritual sacrifice under the old blood covenant as enumerated in Numbers 28. Although this is not an exhaustive list of every type of sacrifice made, listed are some of the sacrifices that were specifically required daily, weekly, monthly and seasonally as follows:

Daily Offering: 2 One-Year Old Lambs without Defect, with 2 Quarts Choice Flour mixed with 1 Quart Pure Oil of Pressed Olives (Burnt Offering) plus a Liquid Offering of 1 Quart of an Alcoholic Beverage with each Lamb. This was to be offered once in the morning and once at night.

Weekly Offering (on the Sabbath): Add to the Daily Offering 2 One-Year Old Lambs without Defect, Grain Offering of 4 Qts Choice Flour moistened with Olive Oil, plus the liquid offering.

Monthly Offering (on the 1st): Daily Offering, Plus Extra Burnt Offering: 2 two young bulls, 1 ram, and 7 one-year-old male lambs, all with no defects; grain offerings of choice flour moistened with olive oil—6 quarts* with each bull, 4 quarts with the ram, 13 and 2 quarts with each lamb; and a liquid offering with each sacrifice: 2 quarts* of wine for each bull, 1/3 of a gallon* for the ram, and 1 quart* for each lamb. AND, 1 male goat for a sin offering to the Lord. This is in addition to the regular burnt offering and its accompanying liquid offering.

Passover Offering: 7 Days of the Monthly Sacrifice + Daily

Just reading this list is exhausting and it doesn't even include the Festival of Harvest, Festival of Trumpets, Day of Atonement, etc. Can you imagine the preparation for and cleanup following each of these sacrifices? Can you fathom the amount of sweat and tears it took to access this much blood on a regular? This was an endless cycle of death. What's more, it was never enough. They had to keep doing the same thing over and over again. Those sacrifices were never meant to last. They were only meant to pave the way for a lasting, permanent solution through grace. That permanent solution of course is Jesus. I cannot say it better than the writer of Hebrews did:

> *The old system under the law of Moses was only a shadow, a dim preview of the good things to come, not the good things themselves. The sacrifices under that system were repeated again and again, year after year, but they were never able to provide perfect cleansing for those who came to worship. If they could have provided perfect cleansing, the sacrifices would have stopped, for the worshipers would have been purified once for all time, and their feelings of guilt would have disappeared. But instead, those sacrifices actually reminded them of their sins year after year. For it is not possible for the blood of bulls and goats to take away sins...*
>
> *For God's will was for us to be made holy by the sacrifice of the body of Jesus Christ, once for all time. Under the old covenant, the priest stands and ministers before the altar day after day, offering the same sacrifices again and again, which can never take away sins. But our High Priest offered himself to God as a single sacrifice for sins, good for all time. Then he sat down in the place of honor at God's right hand.* Hebrews 10:1-4; 10-12 (NLT)

Jesus

I love the way the Message Bible states the superiority of Jesus in comparison to the ritualistic sacrifices of old.

> *Every priest goes to work at the altar each day, offers the same old sacrifices year in, year out, and never makes a dent in the sin problem. As a priest, Christ made a single sacrifice for sins, and that was it! Then he sat down right beside God and waited for his enemies to cave in. It was a perfect sacrifice by a perfect person*

to perfect some very imperfect people. By that single offering, he did everything that needed to be done for everyone who takes part in the purifying process. Hebrews 10:11-14 (NLT)

The transcendence of Jesus over the average priest and His self-sacrifice over that of innumerable sheep and goats is life-changing. What once was a day-in-day-out ritual without hope of completion was done away with in one single sacrificial act. The old system could not even make a dent in sin cancer. The approach was that of long-term treatment of a chronic incurable disease. Then Jesus came, offering Himself as the definitive cure. He was the perfect priest offering the perfect sacrifice and it is through faith in Him alone that we are made perfect! Hallelujah!

In other words, Jesus is enough. Your good works are not enough. The sacrifice of animals is not enough. Living like Mother Theresa is not enough. Faith in Jesus is enough! It is all there is. Out of this faith in Jesus, a new transformative life is born. The New Living Translation states Hebrews 10:14 this way, *For by that one offering he forever made perfect those who are being made holy.*

There is so much that could be said here about Jesus. But, I promised that this would be my version of Cliff's Notes. However, I would be remiss if I did not add just one more tidbit. When it comes to the concept of grace, Jesus is the definition. Jesus is grace personified. But, you don't have to take my word for it. (Shout out to Reading Rainbow.) John words it perfectly in John 1:14, 16-17 NLT:

And the Word became flesh and dwelt among us, and we beheld His glory, the glory as of the only begotten of the Father, full of grace and truth. And of His fullness we have all received, and grace for grace. For the law was given through Moses, but grace and truth came through Jesus Christ.

So you see grace is not a novel concept. It is the point of it all. Grace is the foundation upon which our relationship with God through Christ is built.

CHAPTER SIXTEEN:

GRATIFIED LIFE

There are benefits to this grace relationship that extend far beyond the initial favor granted by the patron. When you are a friend of God through Jesus Christ, there are advantages beyond the ultimate reward of spending eternity with him in heaven. Now that is the gratified life, a life that is rich and satisfying. Our friendship with God comes with so many blessings that I could not begin to exhaust them here. However, let's visit a few just for the sake of understanding why the ultimate patron deserves our highest loyalty and devotion. He is beyond worthy of our faithfulness.

Provision

When we discussed Abraham earlier, we saw that when he was called to sacrifice his only son of promise, Isaac, God stopped him in the nick of time and provided a ram to be sacrificed instead. From that experience, Abraham was inspired to call the mountain, "The Lord Will Provide." He discovered something about who God is that day. I recently heard my father preach a sermon where he illuminated the fact that while Abraham and Isaac were traversing one side of the mountain, God had just what they needed climbing up the other side.

God has a blessing for you and you can't even see it coming, but it is on the way! Sometimes it seems impossible to see how God will provide for you given the circumstances you are in. You simply cannot fathom a way out besides death. But, God has arranged for your provision to be there at the appointed time and place, right when you need it. All you have to do is keep walking in obedience to what God has placed on your heart to do. Faith is the force that will give you the strength to climb the mountain. God's faithfulness is what ensures that everything you need is at the top.

> *What shall we say about such wonderful things as these? If God is for us, who can ever be against us? Since he did not spare even his own Son but gave him up for us all, won't he also give us everything else?* Romans 8:31-32

I love how plainly Paul put this. If God as the ultimate patron gave you the ultimate gift of grace in the person of Jesus Christ, won't He give you everything else you need? If God gave you Jesus, won't He give you a job that will provide for your family and develop your gifts? If God gave you Jesus, won't He give you godly friends that can help support your pursuit of purpose and destiny? If God gave you Jesus, won't He give you everything else? Since God gave you Jesus, you can rest assured that He will supply all of your needs according to His riches in glory by Christ Jesus.

Right now, God is providing for you in ways that are beyond your purview. That is why you cannot give up. You are closer to your blessing than what you even know. Wake up every morning knowing that God knows just what you need and where you need it. Keep pressing on believing that you have the faith to get you to where you need to be and God has just what you need when you get there.

Protection

One's association with the patrons of old would often equate to protection. Think about it, if your enemy recognizes that going to battle with you means going to battle with your patron and all the resources they possess, the enemy will undoubtedly think twice. If the enemy chooses to attack, there is an army of affiliates that come with loyalty to your patron. Understand that God is with you. Whenever you have to fight, you never have to fight alone. This was the understanding that gave David the boldness to step up and accept Goliath's challenge.

David was just a teenager. Goliath was an adult giant that had been studying warfare since his teen years. But, David knew that he was not just fighting for himself or by himself. He was fighting for God's people and God was with him. The Message Bible puts David's faith on display by interpreting 1 Samuel 17:45-47 so plainly:

102

David answered, "You come at me with sword and spear and battle-ax. I come at you in the name of God-of-the-Angel-Armies, the God of Israel's troops, whom you curse and mock. This very day God is handing you over to me. I'm about to kill you, cut off your head, and serve up your body and the bodies of your Philistine buddies to the crows and coyotes. The whole earth will know that there's an extraordinary God in Israel. And everyone gathered here will learn that God doesn't save by means of sword or spear. The battle belongs to God—he's handing you to us on a platter!"

In the Old Testament of the Bible, we see that when God would reveal himself to individuals, they would invent or call him by a name that spoke to that revelation or manifestation or present need. Here, we see David summoning the God-of-the-Angel-Armies. 1 John 4:4 in the New Living Translation says, *But you belong to God, my dear children. You have already won a victory over those people, because the Spirit who lives in you is greater than the spirit who lives in the world.* Victory is yours not because of your own strength, but because of the Spirit who lives in you! Jesus Christ is your protector and your victory in the battle. No matter what the odds look like, you win because you are not alone. The God-of-the-Angel-Armies is with you fighting for you. Hallelujah!

Purpose

For I know the plans I have for you," says the LORD. "They are plans for good and not for disaster, to give you a future and a hope. Jeremiah 29:11 NLT

Maybe you've never heard this before. Perhaps you've heard it, but you did not allow it to really sink in. At this moment, I need you to tune in with every fiber of your being and hear this: God has a purpose and a plan for your life. Contextually, this excerpt was God giving Jeremiah a word for the nation of Israel at large. However, I have no doubt that God has something good in store for you as an individual too! He spoke to Jeremiah about himself individually before He spoke to him about the nation.

The word of the Lord came to me, saying, "Before I formed you in the womb I knew you, before you were born I set you apart; I appointed you as a prophet to the nations."
Jeremiah 1:4-5 NLT

God knew you before you were formed in the womb. God decided that He wanted you for himself before your mother saw your face. God has an appointment for your life! The only difference between you and Jeremiah is the specific nature of his calling, e.g. the era, the geographical location, the assignment. But, just like Jeremiah: (1) God made you. (2) God knows you. (3) God has chosen you.

Peace

You will keep in perfect peace all who trust in you, all whose thoughts are fixed on you! Isaiah 26:3 (NLT)

Just as you may not be able to see the provision God has prepared for you at the top of the mountain, there are times that your circumstances call for at least a level orange alert, sending your mind into a sheer panic. Those times can be one and the same. But, as the friend of God you do not have to panic based on what you do or do not see. Rather than magnifying and meditating on the problem, you can exercise faith by purposefully shifting your thoughts towards the God of all grace that gave you Jesus and will therefore give you everything else. When you shift your thoughts towards that God, you cannot help but to feel better. Better than better, you can have peace if you fix your thoughts on the God who will fix your problems.

I am leaving you with a gift--peace of mind and heart. And the peace I give is a gift the world cannot give. So don't be troubled or afraid. John 14:27

It is up to each one of us not to allow ourselves to be worried and fearful. The grace gift of peace is available to you; but, it is up to you to keep your mind right. Your thoughts will grant you access to the peace of God. I recently heard Christine Caine, a dynamic evangelist and human rights activist say this in a sermon, "I am always only one thought away from my old way of thinking." That old way of thinking will keep you in distress. The old way of thinking makes room for confusion and chaos. Those old thoughts bring drama!

But, God has already given us peace. All we have to do is bring our thoughts in line with faith. Believing that God is and that He will reward you with whatever you need if you diligently seek him is everything. It will keep you from falling apart when it seems like your whole world is doing just that. God has got you and He will keep you.

Just trust him.

Provision, protection, purpose, peace on and on go the benefits of walking in a grace relationship with The Almighty! You cannot have a more gratifying life than what He can provide. It is even more reassuring to know that all of these things are not based on who we are as flawed individuals. It is based on the character of our patron, God the Father and His grace towards us. What are you waiting for? Stop living in angst and unnecessary mental turmoil. It is time to receive the perfect grace of God.

CONCLUSION

In my short lifetime, I have gone from having a complete melt down over a second-grade spelling test, to being able to take one of the most challenging bar exams in the country and almost enjoy the process. I said almost :). I have gone from the constant gnawing of the pain and anxiety that comes with perfectionism and the incessant quest to measure up to a new level of groundedness and comfort in my own skin, despite the pimples and blemishes that come and go. I have gone from feeling like I needed to know all the answers and do everything I can to exercise control over my world to really understanding that I can safely surrender to the God who is in control because He loves and favors me.

While I have not yet arrived, I am so much better. Life is so much better when you are walking freely in the grace of God, not slaving in the shackles of religion, self judgment, and self-reliance. We are not mere servants of God; He called us friend! I want to base the rest of my life on this friendship. It is everything! That is my grace response, to be steadfast, unmovable, totally and absolutely loyal and committed to my grace-based relationship with the Almighty God. Whatever I am, whatever I ever may become, whatever I manage to accomplish, it is all because I have a loving patron who was willing to supply all of my needs according to His riches in glory through Christ Jesus, the ultimate grace gift.

It has been said that "Christianity is one beggar showing another beggar where to find bread." This writing is one mess, telling another mess how to be blessed. It is not about our ability to be good enough. There is no way we can measure up to

God's righteousness. We cannot earn the favor of God. It is all about grace! His grace is available to anyone, no matter your socioeconomic status, race, or level of success. All anyone has to do is go to God, receive the grace and favor He has already provided in Jesus and respond with grace (gratitude and faith).

> *What shall we say about such wonderful things as these? If God is for us, who can ever be against us?* Romans 8:31 (NLT)

Whatever state you may be in at this very moment, know that God is for you. God wants the absolute best for your life. He wants you to win and has already set your victory in motion through His divine favor. He gave you Jesus so rest assured He will give you everything else you need. It really doesn't matter what your world currently looks like. When God demonstrates His grace in your life, things change for the better.

In the creation story, God spoke into the chaos and darkness, the void that became the universe as we know it. In spite of all that the would-be universe was not, The Voice did not reiterate the lack and inadequacy that existed. The Voice did not declare what an obvious mess things were. No! The voice spoke grace over the situation in an echo, "Let there be light."

Let there be light! Let the matter, anti-matter, dark matter, particles atoms and energy come forth from the chaos. Allow the elements that make up this mess, everything that is suppressed into nothing by the dense gravity in an infinitesimally small black hole to come into alignment with The Voice and create something ever expanding from the nothingness. From a darkness so deep that no one else has ever known it, He called forth The Light that would become the foundation of everything in our world.

This gives us hope. If the echoes of grace are powerful enough to spark the creation of everything we know and all we can ever hope to discover out of a chaotic void, imagine what grace at work in us can manifest. Imagine what God's grace can form from the glorious mess that is you. Can I tell you a secret? God has already begun the work in you! As you read the words in this book, and they went from your eyes to the narrator in your head, you heard grace echoing in your soul. That sound is akin to God's voice breaking forth in the heavens making room for light. I hope that you feel illuminated and invigorated by the light of His grace. No matter what you feel, that sound is the catalyst to God creating something amazing out of whatever darkness is in your life.

Now it is your job to respond to grace with grace. God is faithful and worthy of you placing your faith in him. Know that you know that God is able and willing to fulfill His promise to you. If He said it, He will do it! He is so faithful! So believe that at this very moment He is working all things together for your good. Stay in faith. Hold on to the promise and be faithful to the process. The manifestation is on the way.

While you wait, demonstrate gratitude as a lifestyle. Make Jesus famous. Commit to being loyal to the God of the universe. Use your voice and your entire being to praise God. Look for opportunities to give and serve The Ultimate Patron by serving the people around you in church and the greater community. Have confidence in God! Believe that God is and He is a rewarder of them that diligently seek him! Expect something great in your life. Expect God to be faithful to fulfill His word. Finally, enjoy the journey, knowing that no matter how precipitous the path, it is leading you to a future of fulfillment, a rich and satisfying life through a growing relationship with Jesus Christ.

GOD LOVES YOU!!!
(Epilogue)

Maybe this is the first time you have ever heard that. Or, maybe you've heard it a thousand times before and it seems cliché. But, have you ever had a life-changing encounter with the love of God? The fact that God loves you is the most profound truth in the universe. The God who existed before anything else and spoke the earth into being loves you. How do I know this? Because. . .

For God so loved the world that He gave His only begotten Son, that whoever believes in Him should not perish but have everlasting life.
John 3:16 New King James Version

Do You Know It?

If you really knew the love God has for you, your life would radically change. It is impossible to encounter that kind of love and remain indifferent and uninterested. The love and passion that Christ demonstrated on the cross for you provokes a response.

Perhaps you've remained cold and detached as a way to protect yourself from what you think religion is all about. But, this is not about religion; it is about a genuine relationship with the God who created you, knows you intimately and wants nothing more for you than to simply know His love.

Thirst

Jesus went against the social norms of His day and went out of His way to meet a woman at a well. The woman had a bad reputation and braved the heat, getting water at noon just to avoid dealing with the other people in her village. Jesus was waiting for her at just the right time in just the right place.

Defying the prevailing prejudice, Jesus engaged her in conversation. He challenged the way she was living her life religiously, yet continuously trying to quench her own thirst with dysfunctional relationships. It was a vicious cycle that left her unfulfilled and thirsty. Religion was not enough.

Knowing of her thirst, Jesus offered her the living water that would flow from within and provide eternal life. In that moment, she discovered that Jesus was the Messiah, the Christ, the one sent by God to save humanity. She believed in him, her thirst was instantly quenched and she was freed from shame. The woman ran to tell everyone, the same ones she was formerly avoiding, about Jesus. Through hearing her story and seeing her transformation, many came to believe in Jesus.

That is an example of the power of the thirst-quenching love of God that is shown in Christ Jesus towards us.

What About You?

No matter how successful we may be at arranging our lives to minimize or numb any emptiness within, just like that woman we all have a place in our hearts that only God's love can fill. Maybe you've tried to fill it with money, people, or religion. None of those things can quench your thirst. Maybe you didn't realize it until just now, but you are thirsty for an authentic relationship with God through Jesus. We believe that this is the divine time and place that God wants to reveal himself to you.

> *...that Christ may dwell in your hearts through faith; that you, being rooted and grounded in love, may be able to comprehend with all the saints what is the width and length and depth and height — to know the love of Christ which passes knowledge; that you may be filled with all the fullness of God.* Ephesians 3:17-19 King James Version.

This is the Apostle Paul's prayer. His mission in life was to make known the mastery of Christ so that people would put their faith in Him and come to know His God-sized love. This is my prayer for you and your family. The reason you are reading this is because God wants you to discover Christ, put your faith in Him and be filled with His amazing love.

Believe

Whether or not you have warm fuzzy feelings inside, belief is a choice. Choosing to believe in Jesus Christ is the best decision you could ever make. Believing in Jesus is the way to a rich and satisfying life here on earth and to eternal life beyond our present existence.

Sin is a term derived from archery which means "to miss the mark." We've all missed it. That is why we all need a savior.

For all have sinned and fall short of the glory of God.
Romans 3:23 (NLT)

For the wages of sin is death, but the gift of God is eternal life through Jesus Christ our Lord. Romans 6:23 (NLT)

But God demonstrates his own love towards us, in that while we were sinners, Christ died for us. Romans 5:8 (NLT)

If you confess with your mouth the Lord Jesus and believe in your heart that God has raised Him from the dead, you will be saved. Romans 10:9 (NLT)

Are you ready to believe? Pray this prayer out loud: "God, I know I have sinned. But, I believe that You love me so much that you sent Jesus to die for my sins. I believe Jesus rose again so that I can have eternal life. Come into my heart Jesus and be my Lord. Fill me with the Holy Spirit. Thank you Jesus for saving me!

What Next?

1. Go to Church Like Jesus and Get Baptized

Jesus regularly went to church to read the scriptures according to Luke 4:16. Jesus found His identity in the scriptures and was able to overcome temptation by speaking the written truth found in the Bible. Baptism is symbolic of us dying, being buried and raising to new life in Christ according to Romans 6:5. If you have invited Jesus in your heart, then you want to follow His example. To be like Jesus, you need to go to church and get baptized!

2. Tell Someone You Know About Your Decision to Believe in Christ

3. Get to Know Jesus

The point of it all is for you to have an authentic, growing relationship with Jesus. Get closer to him by talking to him (prayer), reading your Bible and attending church.

ABOUT THE AUTHOR

Karen Yvonne Dykes, Esq. is called to communicate transformative truth to encourage, inspire and empower people to live abundantly. She was born and raised in El Paso, TX. She graduated from Hampton University summa cum laude with a degree in Computer Information Systems, having received a full academic scholarship. Karen went on to The University of Texas School of Law where she was awarded a Doctor of Jurisprudence degree. Since then, she has been licensed to practice law in Texas and California and has taken on a myriad of challenges as an Assistant District Attorney, working as an associate at a leading regional firm, and executive pastor. Karen has been known to express her artistic side through song writing and recording, acting and even stand up comedy. However, she is most passionate about her new role as wife and future role as mommy.

Contact:
For booking, further discussion or prayer please contact Karen Yvonne Dykes at karenyvonne7@gmail.com

Facebook:
Karen Yvonne Dykes

Instagram:
Karen Yvonne 7

Twitter:
@karenyvonne7

Made in the USA
Columbia, SC
22 February 2019